Sustainable Finance Fundamentals

Carlos Vargas

Routledge
Taylor & Francis Group

LONDON AND NEW YORK

Designed cover image: © Getty Images

First published 2024
by Routledge
4 Park Square, Milton Park, Abingdon, Oxon OX14 4RN

and by Routledge
605 Third Avenue, New York, NY 10158

Routledge is an imprint of the Taylor & Francis Group, an informa business

British Library Cataloguing-in-Publication Data
A catalogue record for this book is available from the British Library

Library of Congress Cataloging-in-Publication Data
Names: Vargas, Carlos (Professor of finance), author.
Title: Sustainable finance fundamentals/Carlos Vargas.
Description: Abingdon, Oxon; New York, NY: Routledge, 2024. | Includes
bibliographical references and index. | Identifiers: LCCN 2023019103 |
ISBN 9781032229164 (hbk) | ISBN 9781032151489 (pbk) | ISBN 9781003274735 (ebk)
Subjects: LCSH: Finance. | Investments. | Sustainability—Economic aspects.
Classification: LCC HG173 .V35 2024 | DDC 332—dc23/eng/20230719
LC record available at https://lccn.loc.gov/2023019103

ISBN: 978-1-032-22916-4 (hbk)
ISBN: 978-1-032-15148-9 (pbk)
ISBN: 978-1-003-27473-5 (ebk)

DOI: 10.4324/9781003274735

Typeset in Bembo MT Pro
by codeMantra

Access the Support Material: www.routledge.com/9781032151489

Sustainable Finance Fundamentals

Sustainable Finance Fundamentals provides an accessible overview of this critical, rapidly growing area at the intersection of finance and sustainability.

The book showcases different approaches to sustainable finance, covering banking, impact investing, integrated reporting and strategy, and risk management. It covers investing, including equity, green bonds, and crowdfunding. Issues beyond sustainable finance, such as alternative investments, renewable energy, and innovation, are also explored. In addition, two optional appendices provide useful introductions to the time value of money (TVM) and financial statements.

Ethical and regulatory issues are addressed holistically throughout the book and sustainable finance is linked to related topics, such as environmental economics and the UN Sustainable Development Goals. Each chapter has an international focus and features examples, "in a nutshell" summaries, and discussion questions.

Whether you are a student or professional, *Sustainable Finance Fundamentals* is essential reading for anyone looking to gain a comprehensive understanding of sustainable finance, impact investing, and related areas. Lecture slides and teaching notes are also available for instructors, making this book an ideal text for courses on sustainable finance.

Carlos Vargas is Professor of Finance at the EGADE Business School at Tecnologico de Monterrey (Mexico). Dr Vargas has also been instructor of Sustainable Finance in the Division of Continuing Education at Harvard University (USA), the Universidad de los Andes (Colombia), and the University of Zurich (Switzerland), among other prestigious universities all over the world.

Dedication

To every person fighting the good fight who found themselves lost in the details.

Contents

Illustrations

FIGURES

TABLES

Foreword

Thanks for your interest in *Sustainable Finance Fundamentals* (*SFF*). To me, this topic has been an adventure of more than a decade trying to figure out how to make finance more sustainable, but also how to make sustainability profitable. Bridging the gaps between these two very distinct areas has been my area of professional interest since before it was trendy, and I have witnessed how it has evolved to this point.

By writing this book, I know I will step on some toes. I am also mindful that some of the ideas proposed here might be controversial. Honestly, it was never my intention to create a heated piece. Still, I did have a clear goal to be provocative to trigger intellectual curiosity and ultimately drive action. Change begins by acknowledging areas of opportunity, and I sincerely hope that it helps you, dear reader, increase your understanding of this topic. To me, we are not living in a broken system; instead, we are dealing with a system that was designed as it was from the beginning, a system that continues to evolve and has the potential to improve.

My academic and professional experience is by far unconventional. I am not the academic who comes from the library's dark side to design mathematical models that only seem to work under controlled conditions and inside a vacuum. I am pragmatic and practical and am not afraid to guide traffic if needed. This book comes from my first decade of teaching Sustainable Finance in leading academic institutions worldwide, including Harvard University in the United States, Tecnologico de Monterrey in Mexico, the University of Zurich in Switzerland, and Universidad de los Andes in Colombia.

HOW TO USE THIS BOOK?

This book is divided into five sections (including the appendix) for our readers' convenience. First, you will find the introduction. There you will find basic concepts and a general understanding of what sustainable finance is and how it came to be. In the second section, different approaches to sustainable finance, you will find a compendium of chapters that cover the idea of value and valuation, as well as three others that cover how the financial industry deals with SF. Different asset classes are introduced in the third section, Investing in and Financing Sustainable Finance. And the concepts of sustainability indices and crowdfunding are also covered. The fourth section, Going beyond Sustainable Finance Fundamentals, deals with the energy transition, carbon markets, and other alternative assets and concludes with innovation. Then in the appendix, you may find additional content that complements the ideas mentioned in the book, containing an introduction to TVM and financial statements.

I wrote a book that is easy to read but also provides a helpful resource for those interested in this topic. It is written and structured to be fluid and as complete and comprehensive as possible. I advise you to give this full manuscript an opportunity before building a critical perception. If possible, read it all in order. There is a reason for the choice of topics and the order in which they are presented; perhaps you can benefit from all that. However, this book can also be a good reference piece for more practical readers.

I hope you enjoy this book, and thanks again for joining me on the journey of learning about sustainable finance.

Dr. Carlos Vargas
Author

Acronyms and definitions

°C	Degrees Celsius
AI	Artificial Intelligence
ATM	Automated Teller Machine
AUM	Assets under Management
BIS	Bank of International Settlements
CBA	Cost–Benefit Analysis
CBI	Climate Bond Initiative
CDM	Clean Development Mechanism
CO_2	Carbon Dioxide
COP	Conference of the Parties
DCF	Discounted Cash Flow
DJIA	Dow Jones Industrial Average Index
EC	European Commission
EP	Equator Principles
EPC	Engineering, Procurement, and Construction
ESG	Environmental, Social, and Governance
ESPC	Energy Savings Performance Contracting
ETF	Exchange Traded Fund
ETS	Emission Trading System
EU	European Union
Fintech	Financial Technology Company
FIT	Feed-in Tariff
FV	Future Value
GAAP	Generally Accepted Accounting Principles
GHG	Greenhouse Gas
GIIN	Global Impact Investing Network
GSS+	Green Social and Sustainable Bond, and Others
i.e.	In example
ICMA	ICMA International Capital Market Association
IFRS	International Financial Reporting Standards
IPCC	Intergovernmental Panel on Climate Change
ISSB	International Sustainability Standards Board

IT	Information and Technology
KPI	Key Performance Indicators
LIBOR	The London Inter-Bank Offered Rate
MPG	Miles per Gallon
NPV	Net Present Value
PE	Private Equity
PES	Payment for Environmental Services
Ph.D.	Doctor of Philosophy
PPA	Power Purchase Agreement
PPP	People, Planet, and Profit
PRI	Principles of Responsible Investment
PV	Present Value
R&D	Research and Development
RE	Real Estate
REIT	Real Estate Investment Trust
SAM	Sustainable Asset Management
SBG	Sustainability Bond Guidelines
SBP	Social Bond Principles
SBTi	Science-Based Targets
SDG	Sustainable Development Goals
SEC	US Securities and Exchange Commission
SF	Sustainable Finance
SLB	Sustainability-Linked Bonds
SLBP	Sustainability-Linked Bonds Principles
SLL	Sustainability-Linked Loan
SLLP	Sustainability-Linked Loans Principles
SP500	Standard and Poor's 500 Index
SPT	Sustainability Performance Targets
SRE	Sustainable Real Estate
SRI	Sustainable and Responsible Investments
SSF	Swiss Sustainable Finance
TBL	Triple Bottom Line
TBTF	Too Big to Fail Corporations
TVM	Time Value of Money
UN	United Nations
UNEP	UN Environment Program
UNFCCC	United Nations Framework Convention on Climate Change
WEF	World Economic Forum
WWF	World Wildlife Fund

CHAPTER 1

Introduction

WHAT IS SUSTAINABLE FINANCE?

Sustainable finance (SF) is one vibrant and exciting area of finance. It embodies the complexity of different ideas and implementations, and we will navigate them to better understand what it contains. SF is a topic that seems fresh and cutting-edge in general. Still, it has been around for some years, so we will also describe its evolution and explore its actual aims and objectives.

In Figure 1.1, we can see how SF is a subset of finance, as it aims to pursue environmental, social, and governance (ESG) factors and impact together with return to different degrees. As far as we can strictly define SF, it is part of finance, but it is not like traditional finance that centers decision-making on financial return as a priority. But SF is a complex term to define. It may depend on whom you ask and the sort of definition that you might find in many cases. It also may go by different names, i.e., green finance, microcredit, socially responsible investments, green bonds, impact investments, ESG, etc., which in most cases are just subsets of SF. But getting lost in the terminology is easy, so let us review some definitions of SF by different global organizations: i.e., the United Nations (UN), European Commission (EC), and Swiss Sustainable Finance (SSF). All of them have their take on this term, and it is relevant to consider them as global trailblazers of this terminology.

UNITED NATIONS

Our first two definitions come from different areas of the UN. Given that the UN is such a relevant and substantial institution, we can observe how both definitions, one from the UN Environment Programme (UNEP) and the other from the World Wildlife Fund (WWF), align significantly, showing a sort of agreement on the term.

> At WWF, we believe that a sustainable financial system is one that accounts for its environmental, social, and economic impacts over the short, medium, and long term in all its investment and lending decisions and encourages the positive social and environmental development of society.
>
> (Mugglin, Rendlen, Favier, & Frey, 2017)

DOI: 10.4324/9781003274735-1

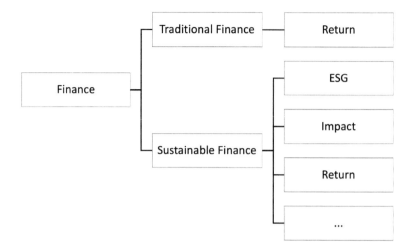

FIGURE 1.1 SF as a subset of finance.

We can also find the definition by UNEP as follows:

> Green financing increases the level of financial flows (from banking, micro-credit, insurance, and investment) from the public, private, and not-for-profit sectors to sustainable development priorities. A vital part of this is to manage environmental and social risks better, take up opportunities that bring a decent rate of return and ecological benefit, and deliver greater accountability.
>
> (UN Environment Programme, n.d.)

As we can see, the WWF focuses more on the environmental, social, and economic parts for the short, medium, and long term and introduces the concept of "system" as part of their definition. Also, it includes lending and investment as part of the concept, while the UNEP clearly focuses on financing and covers different examples of financial solutions that arise from it. Risks are then accounted for, which is novel to this point, and we then find a goal, "a decent rate of return and ecological benefit," in other words, return and impact. And finally it introduces the concept of accountability, which we will get back to further in the book. The two definitions seem to align but also complement each other. They show interesting highlights on what SF should be, but we can also check other views.

EUROPEAN COMMISSION

For the European Commission (EC), SF is a process that is defined as follows:

> Sustainable finance refers to the process of taking environmental, social, and Governance (ESG) considerations into account when making investment decisions in the financial sector, leading to more long-term investments in sustainable economic activities and projects. Environmental concerns might include climate change mitigation and adaptation

and the environment more broadly, for instance, the preservation of biodiversity, pollution prevention, and the circular economy. Social considerations could refer to inequality, inclusiveness, labor relations, human capital and community investment, and human rights issues. The Governance of public and private institutions – including management structures, employee relations, and executive remuneration – plays a fundamental role in ensuring the inclusion of social and environmental considerations in the decision-making process.

(European Commission, n.d.-b)

In the EC context, a relevant concept to include is governance, and if we read carefully, "long-term" is somehow highlighted in this definition. Several new concepts, including "human rights" and "biodiversity," are also introduced. In general terms, the EC defines SF as a process that supports economic growth while reducing the risks that ESG represents. Although risks are not precisely called as such in this definition, we rather find terms such as "concerns." It is also relevant to mention that in this definition, the concept of financial and corporate actors is introduced as we find repeated mention of decision-making.

SWISS SUSTAINABLE FINANCE

One definition that I like is from SSF. It seems to be very concrete with regard to the basics.

"Sustainable finance refers to any form of financial service integrating environmental, social and governance (ESG) criteria into the business or investment decisions for the lasting benefit of both clients and society at large"

(Swiss Sustainable Finance, n.d.).

This definition covers the diversity of applications of the general concept and ventures into ESG criteria. It also goes as far as to say the lasting benefits for society and clients. Still, it does fail to integrate other interpretations, such as accountability, materiality, and risk, that are usually included.

Finding a definition for SF

Defining SF can be puzzling as there are few standard definitions. Although different geographies, corporations, and organizations may use similar terminologies, we do not find perfect agreement on it. And sometimes, even the same language can mean different things. For me, a good definition would define what finance is and incorporate what that sustainability part of finance should be according to the systems perspective, as follows: "Sustainable Finance is the system that ponders a holistic approach to material ESG considerations and impact when making decisions in investing, and lending with the intention to create sustained value and manage risk in the long-term."

By such a definition, particular criteria not included specifically can be contained as a holistic approach, and this definition is somehow less prescriptive but ends up being more inclusive. SF should also somehow refer to intentionality and be a process that is aware, conscious, and proactive, and that somehow can also be included in the definition – but this is just a modest proposal, and of course, if there was a perfect definition, we would have already found it.

Green, ESG criteria, and other applications should be part of these definitions somehow. They are included by using wider terms, such as "holistic." But no matter how far we go to list aspects of SF, as this is still an evolving field, the list would never be comprehensive. We would have to cover many things in a categorized order, and we will see different examples in the following chapters. And in any case, we cannot ignore the relevance of agreeing to a general "taxonomy," a term we must still define but that falls on the regulatory side of things and should eventually prevent undesirable practices, such as greenwashing, which we will discuss in this work.

And talking about regulation, we will also find a space to discuss it further later in this book, from the perspective of both the EC[1] in Europe and the Securities and Exchange Commission (SEC)[2] in the United States, which are the main players in regulation. Different regulators recognize the role of ESG criteria in finance and indicate interest, particularly to disclosure, as the agenda advances everywhere. However, coming to this point, we will try to stick to the task of defining the concept of SF.

WHERE ARE WE TODAY REGARDING SF?

Perhaps interest in the topic of SF started to simmer even early, but it sure started to show more clearly at the beginning of the second decade of the 21st century. We already knew about the historical urgency to face the effects of climate change and everything that the growing interest in sustainability may have represented until that moment, but goals set for 2030 and 2050 did not seem as distant as they silently appeared to be closer than expected. Time went fast, and we started to discuss climate change at the first COP (Conference of the Parties) meeting in Berlin, Germany, in March 1995 (United Nations Climate Change, n.d.-a); however, not much had been solved in 27 more meetings by the time this book was written.

After the pandemic, some of us had the opportunity to reflect upon ourselves and what others that came before we did, and we chose to do it better. Once younger generations came of age to speak their minds and become decision-makers, to question a world that they did not do much harm to but pretty much dwelt in and would inherit later. Remember Greta Thunberg, a 16-year-old Swedish activist talking about "a house on fire" at the World Economic Forum (WEF) (Thunberg, 2019), when referring to the urgency to take action regarding climate change. We still had the chance to start doing something about climate change, inequity, injustices, and so many pressing issues, and we chose to start. We have a historical challenge ahead of us, perhaps the most significant challenge humanity has ever faced. We will have to find solutions in all human influence and activity areas. And somehow there, with all this new awareness and urgency, we see a place to reflect on what finance does and how it aligns with those aims and needs.

Perhaps 2020 was the perfect example of the fragility and inflexibility of our financial system. A small virus was able to upset the world economy and in just six months we lost almost all the jobs created in the decade since the last economic crisis. Now imagine what an uncontrolled rise in sea level or the occurrence of evermore frequent 100-year storms that typically occur every 100 years, but now occur every other year, could signify. The list of potential perils goes on, and that is only on the environmental side. And that is not even half of the story as we also have to keep in mind the social side of finance. We also need to mind how unfair and unequal our decisions within the financial system are. We urge everyone to bridge racial, gender, and other social gaps with urgency. And we hear the calls for attention from almost everyone almost every day, but things change slowly. Perhaps we believed that the economy could be the panacea to solve every problem. We trusted the economy to grow and self-regulate to be the solution, but we were relying on general assumptions that sometimes work only under controlled conditions, something that is, at best, the opposite of real life. So we urged a new paradigm, one that included environmental and social impacts and value creation. That is the paradigm that allows for the ideation of SF. And so, we start to question the very essence of finance.

HOW DID WE GET THERE?

Some people believe that SF is a new topic. Still, as others describe (Weber & Feltmate, 2018), its actual origin can be traced back to the 16th century when Italian banks constructed their business on religious ethics to finance local businesses. A more recent background for this field emerged in the 1960s with the start of the environmental movement (Carson, 1962) and in the 1970s with the grounding of ethical banks, and it was followed by the early stages of ESG approaches in the 1980s. But it was not until the 1990s that SF was more established as a concept, and some other subfields, such as carbon finance and impact investment, started to emerge. Nevertheless, it was only after 2008, after the advent of the financial crisis, that many countries started to develop a new understanding of the financial industry.

We can also mention that more substantial efforts or initiatives have been undertaken since 1992. UNEP-FI, the United Nations Environment Programme, Finance Initiative, was established in that year and was defined as a partnership between the United Nations Environment and the global financial sector. They defined their mission to promote SF and have over 230 financial institutions as members. In their words, they "work with UN Environment to understand today's environmental, social and governance challenges, why they matter to finance, and how to participate in addressing them actively."[3] The Equator Principles (EP),[4] established later in 2003, were also a relevant effort along a similar route. They were set as a risk management framework for financial institutions. And they aimed to determine, assess, and manage environmental and social risk in project finance and provided a minimum standard for due diligence to support responsible risk decision-making. The Principles of Responsible Investment (PRI)[5] came later in 2006 to recognize ESG criteria. It went a bit further by establishing a support network for its international signatories to promote the incorporation of ESG criteria into investment and ownership decisions. Other initiatives, such as the Global Impact Investing Network (GIIN),[6] founded a year after, aimed to reduce barriers to impact investment. They develop and provide infrastructure and developing activities, education, and research to accelerate the development of a coherent impact investing industry. And several others have followed. As can be noticed, these actors in the SF field have aimed to establish networks and a support system. They have developed additional new concepts to define further this field's scope, i.e., impact investment.

WHAT IS THE ACTUAL AIM OF SF?

SF as a subject for academic study is perhaps more novel. This discipline includes different factors as building blocks and sometimes also had and touched other academic subfields, i.e., corporate social responsibility, ethics, and governance. This subject was introduced just recently as a business curriculum at the university level, but now it is possible to find Master Programs that offer majors and minors in SF, and even some Ph.D. programs; however, the scope and even the literature and research that exists in this discipline, although it continues to grow, is still limited. SF, however, has gained relevance at an accelerated pace due to the need to adapt to complex global conditions and the interest of governments, companies, organizations, and individuals in sustainability.

Climate change has also been a cornerstone of this field. The notion of climate change, which began a couple of decades ago as a topic of debate and controversy, is now a determining factor for many industries and is becoming increasingly difficult to ignore. Moreover, 100-year storms happening almost every year led us to provide for climate risks that historically we were not even ready to face. Even Dow Jones has a sustainability index now. Different actors in the financial world have started to offer services and products that can be regarded as sustainable to various degrees. This offer responds to the interest of investors, who see that these issues have begun to transcend the concept of the trend to become the new corporate standard. Virtually all financial institutions around the globe now cater to investment options that include sustainability as an investment criterion. These and many other examples involve the environment of SF.

SF is a holistic conception of the study of return based on the risk that does not ignore the traditional concepts of valuation and resource management of conventional finance but complements and updates those concepts incorporating valuation measures of environmental and social aspects, as part of their risk measurement and mitigation strategies. Methodologies such as hedonic valuation, cost-benefit analysis, or payment for environmental services allow the establishment of new parameters for a better-valued and efficient real estate industry. Thousands of companies worldwide use these and many other valuation methodologies to capture value in their investments.

WHAT IS NOT SF?

SF finds momentum to advance all over the world. SF ensures and improves economic efficiency, prosperity, and economic competitiveness both in the short and in the long term, while contributing to protecting and restoring ecological systems and enhancing cultural diversity and social well-being (Swiss Sustainable Finance, n.d.). As we can observe, ESG criteria seem to have established standards, but their interpretation and assessment cannot be easily defined either.

And some generally agreed-upon activities fall under SF, i.e., renewable energy, development, green bonds, impact investing, microfinance, green real estate, etc. This work mainly contributes to studying the first two activities listed above. Perhaps the ESG component, or as some others call it, impact, could be the differential component between SF and convention

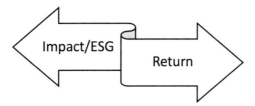

FIGURE 1.2 Impact/ESG and return as two opposing prongs.

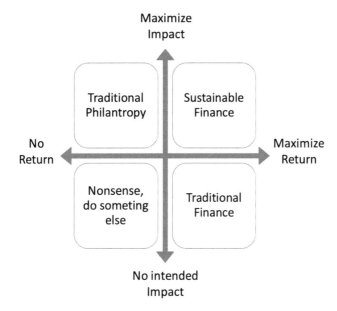

FIGURE 1.3 SF, traditional finance, and philanthropy according to return and impact orientation.

finance. Nevertheless, what about charity and philanthropy, which aim to have a social and sometimes environmental impact. Weber and Feltmate propose an interesting idea to establish how this could be determined (Weber & Feltmate, 2018).

Figure 1.2 shows how impact and ESG can sometimes seem opposites to return, highlighting the common misconception that SF is costly and not profitable for companies. This is not accurate, as we will describe further in this book how SF can create value directly and reduce risk to create value indirectly. In Figure 1.3, however, as we introduce different dimensions of assessment, we can observe how SF, traditional finance, and philanthropy can coexist. This stylized representation shows how both financial return and impact are aimed in two different dimensions. An excellent SF implementation would target both goals and not determine a trade-off between them. Meanwhile, traditional finance would always forgo impact with the aim of financial return, while philanthropy would prioritize its impact mandate.

This fact contradicts the conception of Freedman, as published in his 1970s essay in the *New York Times Magazine*[7] entitled "The Social Responsibility of Business Is to Increase Its Profits," and the piece delivered well as per its title. In his view, "social responsibility" to the public or society for corporations is limited to increasing profits for its shareholders (Friedman, 1970). Or in other words, the business of business is business. That traditional view of finance from the 1970s has been embedded in regulation for decades to follow and is currently challenged by the very concept of SF. A lot, and even the very conception of what business should be or do, has changed in the last 50 years or so. Businesses should be profitable, but that is not the only criterion. They need to show profit sustainably. They can even be seen as a "powerful instrument of change," as described by Rodin and Brandenburg (2014). But just as businesses should yield more than return, SF is not philanthropy either. Philanthropy is a very successful model to support good causes, but it is generally sponsored by donations, and SF is a for-profit effort. All three categories are needed and have different aims, but they can be clearly differentiated, as we can see in Figure 1.3.

EVOLUTION OF SF

In a famous quote by Adam Smith, we hear about the essence of traditional finance: "It is not from the benevolence of the butcher, the brewer, or the baker that we expect our dinner, but from their regard to their self-interest" (Smith, 1998). Perhaps we have all heard this quote by Adam Smith (1723–1790), who is considered by many the father of economics, and some go even further to say he might be the father of capitalism. I guess he can say enough by reading the above quote. His influence in classical economics and finance cannot be denied. But his regard for self-interest at the center of the economic system is perhaps one of the biggest mis-understandings in economics. Humans are, in essence, pro-social, and although self-interest is inherent to human nature, it is not the only trait we regard.

On the other side, we have the celebrated Milton Friedman (1912–2006), an American economist who was awarded the Nobel Memorial Prize in Economic Sciences in 1976. He was perhaps most known for his work on the economy, and some of his contributions are well-regarded in the field. He published on September 13, 1970, an essay for the *New York Times* that we have described above.

We have come a long way from corporate social responsibility to where we are today in SF. And perhaps some of the foundations of modern economics and, therefore, finance are based on simplifications that, at the time they were conceived, were easier to model and estimate. Technology has advanced significantly, and our understanding of the world we live in has also advanced considerably in the last decades.

We need to understand the evolution of SF as a live form. We can go from the general under-standing of traditional finance, only trying to maximize profit and have a short-term horizon in mind. And start considering the first steps into an organized knowledge of SF through exclu-sion and early approaches to incorporating ESG aspects. Authors like Schoenmaker conceive this evolution as going from SF 1.0 to SF 3.0. The former, SF 1.0, is an early understanding of refined shareholder value, but still with a short-term perspective. SF 2.0 is based on the under-standing of what has been defined as the triple bottom line (TBL) but aiming to optimize value in the medium term. Meanwhile, SF 3.0 aims to find common good value, optimizing social and environmental factors for creating value in the long term (Schoenmaker, 2017).

OTHER RELEVANT NOTIONS

To build up our understanding of these basic ideas and concepts, we need to define some relevant basic concepts.

TRIPLE BOTTOM LINE

The TBL is the understanding in finance and economics that investors and companies should focus beyond the financial bottom line, profit. And so environmental and social factors are also defined as bottom lines to include them in the assessment. This is also commonly known as planet, people, and profit or PPP, as shown in Figure 1.4. And so, the TBL purpose of measuring the financial, social, and environmental performance of a company over time. John Elkington first introduced this concept in 1994 (Elkington, 1997), but 25 years later retired the concept officially to rethink on it (Elkington, 2018). To some, implementing the TBL approach turns out to be idealistic as we tend to emphasize profit over purpose. Innovation, however, opens the possibility of finding schemes to do well by doing good.

But still, we could do a bit more, as perhaps PPP should rather be understood as concentric circles, as proposed by Kate Raworth in Doughnut Economics. (Raworth, 2017). Figure 1.5 represents this. If we think about it, this makes more sense.

TAXONOMIES

Taxonomies are referenced a lot in SF literature, and they are basically a classification system that defines what is green or environmentally sustainable and what is not. Just as simple as that. And it is commonly accepted that when properly designed, SF taxonomies can deliver potential benefits for the market. According to the Bank of International Settlements (BIS), "sustainable finance taxonomies can play an important role in scaling up sustainable finance and, in turn, in supporting the achievement of high-level goals such as the Paris Accord and the UN sustainable development goals" (Ehlers, Gao, & Pack, 2021). Originally the term taxonomy comes from biology and refers to the classification systems used to organize organisms, but perhaps it goes beyond our point here.

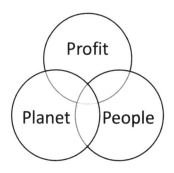

FIGURE 1.4 Elements of the TBL in no particular order.

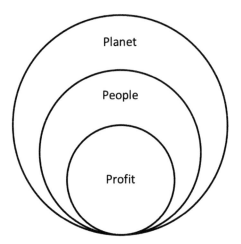

FIGURE 1.5 Elements of the TBL as three concentric circles.

For the European Union (EU), taxonomies have allowed us to find a common language and a clear definition of "sustainable" as regulation is more advanced and requires such level of detail, and they called it "EU taxonomy."

The EU taxonomy is a catalog listing environmentally sustainable economic activity. The EU taxonomy allows companies, investors, and policymakers to find appropriate definitions for which economic activities can be considered environmentally sustainable. This provides clarity to the market and prevents greenwashing, among other goals.

Just to elaborate a bit more, the EU Taxonomy Regulation (European Commission, n.d. a,) establishes six objectives:

1   *Climate change mitigation*
2   *Climate change adaptation*
3   *The sustainable use and protection of water and marine resources*
4   *The transition to a circular economy*
5   *Pollution prevention and control*
6   *The protection and restoration of biodiversity and ecosystems*

In recent years, the concepts of sustainability and green taxonomies have gained significant attention worldwide. Several countries have been actively working towards the development and implementation of policies and initiatives aimed at promoting sustainable practices and investment in green sectors. In Latinamerica, countries, such as Mexico, and Colombia, have made notable progress in establishing green taxonomies and sustainable finance frameworks, which provide clear guidelines for identifying environmentally friendly and socially responsible investments. But countries in other regions are also following closely.

GREENWASHING

Financial greenwashing is to communicate false or misleading statements to exploit the false impression that a financing instrument is environmentally friendly or sustainable. Greenwashing can be either intentional or unintentional, due to the complexity of environmental data, but it is no less severe as it impairs the market. Greenwashing can cause harm in different ways, but it usually reflects in at least one of the following two forms:

1 Reputational damage: Customers discover false claims and unethical practices that lead to a loss of trust and credibility.
2 Environmental damage: By misleading customers and companies, the vicious cycle of inaction continues and halts environmental progress.

Vagueness and ambiguity can also be greenwashing. In fact, any inaccurate, false, or misleading information can yield greenwashing, and responsible parties to that information are accountable for it. That is one of the reasons why regulation is urgently needed in SF, as it has become a growing field. Social washing can also exist in similar terms when social factors are misrepresented and/or forged, but it can also be included in the general term of greenwashing.

DIFFERENT STAKEHOLDERS, ROLES, AND ARENAS

There is so much that can be approached by the work of corporations and individuals toward a more sustainable world, but there is also so much that governments should do. None of them can solve this challenge by themselves. Solving a global challenge requires coordination. On one side, politicians should regulate to set a common ground for more sustainable practices. Still, they also need to be cautious not to overregulate and end up with a bigger problem than they originally wanted to solve.

At the same time, corporations and individuals can also play their part and make better choices. Corporations on their side can make sure that they comply with the best practices of sustainability and be transparent in disclosing their activities and their impacts. Corporations need to create value sustainably. Individuals on their side have the right and responsibility to be informed. So they can also make the best decision regarding their consumption, for which they should be responsible. That is what coordination means in raw terms. Coordination is required to find actual strengths through synergies with everyone playing their role. And that is an exciting point to start with, but it does not mean we are even there yet. Almost every participant in this global market believes that they are doing their part, not willing to forgo anything else to get it better. And we already know that it is not working. Yes, it does help, but we still need to do more.

We even have a goal not to keep an increase below 2°C (United Nations Climate Change, n.d.-b). We are already beyond that, but that initial aim was not reasonable, to begin with. Yet many scientists agree that the goal should have been 1.5°C; it was more a political and diplomatic compromise to set it at 2°C. But the world will not be defined by our standards, even if we are too stubborn to understand. And I do understand how that way of thinking is embedded deep into most of us. But we urge a new way of thinking if we want to solve something we helped create with our previous mindsets and dogmas. Everything we do helps, but we can undoubtedly coordinate better and do more. We are all relevant parts of this solution, as shown in Figure 1.6, but it takes a town.

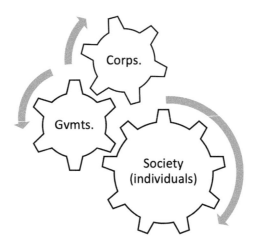

FIGURE 1.6 Society (individuals), corporations, and governments as key gears in solving climate change.

IN A NUTSHELL

We live in a vibrant world that continually changes by leaps and bounds. In fact, more recently, we started to experience an ideological revolution where what seemed to be the norm for decades is rapidly replaced by new ideas and concepts of reality. Changes are driven by need, and for SF a lot started with the notion of climate change, perhaps even in the 1960s, but the urgency came later, much more recently, maybe because of a pandemic and everything that turned paradigms upside down, or maybe because we finally realized the size of the drawback that we were confronting. In any case, SF is the new normal for the financial world, and it is no longer a trend, but it is here to stay.

DISCUSSION QUESTIONS

1   What is the difference between traditional finance and sustainable finance?
2   How has the concept of sustainable finance evolved over the years?
3   What are some examples of financial solutions that arise from sustainable finance?
4   How can sustainable finance help address environmental and social challenges, such as climate change and inequality?
5   What are some of the pressing issues that humanity is facing today that require solutions in all human influence and activity areas?
6   How did the pandemic reveal the fragility and inflexibility of our financial system?
7   What is the actual aim of sustainable finance, and how does it differ from traditional finance?
8   What is the triple bottom line, and how is it relevant to sustainable finance?
9   What is the EU taxonomy, and how does it prevent greenwashing in sustainable finance?
10 What role can corporations and individuals play regarding the implementation of sustainable finance?

NOTES

1 For further information, see https://commission.europa.eu/
2 For further information, see https://www.sec.gov/
3 For further reference, see https://www.unepfi.org/
4 For further reference, see https://equator-principles.com/
5 For further reference, see https://www.unpri.org/
6 For further reference, see https://thegiin.org/
7 To see the full text, go to https://www.nytimes.com/1970/09/13/archives/a-friedman-doctrine-the-social-responsibility-of-business-is-to.html

WORKS CITED

Carson, R. (1962). *Silent spring*. Houghton Mifflin Harcour.

Ehlers, T., Gao, D., & Pack, F. (2021). *BIS Papers No 118 A taxonomy of sustainable finance taxonomies*. Bank for International Settlements. Retrieved from bis.org/publ/bppdf/bispap118.pdf

Elkington, J. (1997). The triple bottom line. In M. Russo (Ed.), *Environmental management: Readings and cases* (2nd ed., pp. 49–66). SAGE Publications

Elkington, J. (2018, June 25). 25 years ago I coined the phrase "Triple Bottom Line." Here's why it's time to rethink it. *Harvard Business Review*.

European Commission. (n.d.-a). *EU taxonomy for sustainable activities*. Retrieved from https://finance.ec.europa.eu/sustainable-finance/tools-and-standards/eu-taxonomy-sustainable-activities_en

European Commission. (n.d.-b). *Overview of sustainable finance*. Retrieved from https://ec.europa.eu/info/business-economy-euro/banking-and-finance/sustainable-finance/overview-sustainable-finance_en

Friedman, M. (1970, September 13). Responsibility of business is to increase its profits. *The New York Times*.

Mugglin, I., Rendlen, B., Favier, A., & Frey, N. (2017). *WWF white paper: Sustainable finance – now or never!* WWF Switzerland.

Raworth, K. (2017). *Doughnut economics: Seven ways to think like a 21st-century economist*. Chelsea Green Publishing.

Rodin, J., & Brandenburg, M. (2014). *The power of impact investing: Putting markets to work for profit and global good*. Wharton School Press.

Schoenmaker, D. (2017). *From risk to opportunity: A framework for sustainable finance*. Rotterdam School of Management series on positive change 2. Rotterdam School of Management, Erasmus University.

Smith, A. (1998). *An inquiry into the nature and causes of the wealth of nations: A selected edition*. Oxford University Press.

Swiss Sustainable Finance. (n.d.). *What is Sustainable Finance*. Retrieved from https://www.sustainablefinance.ch/en/what-is-sustainable-finance-_content---1--1055.html

Thunberg, G. (2019, January 25). This article is more than 3 years old 'Our house is on fire': Greta Thunberg, 16, urges leaders to act on climate. *The Guardian*. Retrieved from https://www.theguardian.com/environment/2019/jan/25/our-house-is-on-fire-greta-thunberg16-urges-leaders-to-act-on-climate

UN Environment Programme. (n.d.). *Green financing*. Retrieved from https://www.unep.org/regions/asia-and-pacific/regional-initiatives/supporting-resource-efficiency/green-financing

United Nations Climate Change. (n.d.-a). *Conference of the Parties (COP)*. Retrieved from https://unfccc.int/process/bodies/supreme-bodies/conference-of-the-parties-cop

United Nations Climate Change. (n.d.-b). *Key aspects of the Paris Agreement*. Retrieved from https://unfccc.int/most-requested/key-aspects-of-the-paris-agreement

Weber, O., & Feltmate, B. (2018). *Sustainable banking*. University of Toronto Press.

CHAPTER 2

Value creation through sustainable finance

WHAT IS VALUATION?

Financial valuation refers to the process of determining the value of an asset, investment, or business. The primary goal of financial valuation is to arrive at a fair estimate of an asset's intrinsic value, which is the true worth of the asset based on its current and future cash flows. This process is essential for investors, business owners, and financial analysts who want to make informed decisions about buying or selling an asset, investing in a business, or assessing the financial health of a company (Koller, Goedhart, & Wessels, 2010).

There are various methods of financial valuation, each with its strengths and weaknesses. Some of the most commonly used methods include discounted cash flow (DCF) analysis, comparable company analysis, and precedent transaction analysis. DCF analysis involves estimating the future cash flows of an asset and discounting them back to their present value using a discount rate that reflects the risk associated with the investment. Comparable company analysis involves comparing the financial metrics of a company to those of similar companies in the same industry to arrive at a valuation. Precedent transaction analysis involves looking at the prices paid for similar assets in previous transactions to determine an asset's value.

SHORT-TERM AND LONG-TERM VALUE CREATION

Short-term value creation refers to the creation of value that has an immediate impact on a company's financial performance, often within a year or less. This value creation is focused on maximizing profits in the short term, such as increasing revenue, reducing costs, or improving margins. It is usually measured by financial metrics such as quarterly earnings, stock price, or cash flow.

Long-term value creation, on the other hand, refers to the creation of value that has a lasting impact on a company's performance over a longer period, often beyond a year. This value creation is focused on sustainable growth, innovation, and competitive advantage. It may involve investments in R&D, brand building, talent development, or capital expenditures that enhance a company's strategic positioning. It is typically measured by non-financial metrics such as customer satisfaction, market share, or employee engagement.

DOI: 10.4324/9781003274735-2

While short-term value creation is important for a company's immediate financial health and stability, long-term value creation is essential for its sustained success and competitiveness in the marketplace. Companies that focus only on short-term value creation may neglect important investments in innovation, brand building, or employee development that are critical for long-term success. Conversely, companies that focus exclusively on long-term value creation may fail to meet short-term financial targets, which can negatively impact their stakeholders and their ability to invest in long-term value creation. A balanced approach that considers both short-term and long-term value creation is necessary for a company's success.

SHORT-TERMISM

Short-termism is a business strategy that focuses on maximizing immediate gains and short-term financial performance at the expense of long-term sustainability and growth. This approach is often characterized by a lack of investment R&D, talent development, and other initiatives that may not show immediate returns (Dallas, 2011; Marginson & McAulay, 2008).

Companies should avoid short-termism for several reasons:

Limited growth potential: A focus on short-term results can lead to missed opportunities for long-term growth and innovation. Companies that fail to invest in R&D, for example, may not be able to develop new products or services that can drive future growth.

Reduced competitive advantage: Companies that prioritize short-term gains over long-term strategic positioning may sacrifice their competitive advantage. Competitors that invest in long-term initiatives, such as employee development, may ultimately outperform companies that prioritize short-term results.

In addition to the more obvious or direct reasons, short-termism can have two more negative and perhaps less obvious consequences. First, it can damage relationships with stakeholders such as employees, customers, and investors, as companies that prioritize short-term gains may cut corners on product quality, leading to dissatisfied customers. Second, it can lead to decisions that prioritize profits over the well-being of society and the environment, as companies may engage in unsustainable practices to maximize short-term gains, leading to negative environmental or social impact.

To avoid short-termism, companies should adopt a long-term mindset and invest in initiatives that drive sustainable growth and innovation. This may involve taking calculated risks, developing a strong company culture, and communicating transparently with stakeholders about long-term goals and strategies.

TANGIBLE AND INTANGIBLE VALUE

Tangible value refers to something that can be physically touched, seen, or measured. Examples of tangible value include real estate, machinery, inventory, or cash. Intangible value, on the other hand, refers to something that cannot be physically touched or seen but can still have value. Examples of intangible value include brand reputation, customer loyalty, intellectual property, or human capital. While tangible value is more easily quantifiable, intangible value

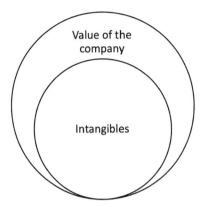

FIGURE 2.1 A stylized representation of the value of intangibles as part of the value of a company.

can also be important in determining the overall value of a company or asset (Figure 2.1). For example, a company with a strong brand reputation may have a higher value than a company with similar tangible assets but a weaker reputation (Eisfeldt, Kim, & Papanikolaou, 2020).

HOW TO CREATE LONG-TERM VALUE?

Creating long-term value in a company involves focusing on sustainable growth and competitive advantage. There are many ways by which this goal can be promoted. Here are some examples.

Long-term investment horizons

A long-term investment horizon refers to a strategy where investors hold their investments for an extended period, typically over five years. Long-term investment horizons are popular among investors who are looking for stable returns and are willing to withstand short-term volatility in exchange for potentially higher returns over the long run. The advantage of a long-term investment horizon is that it allows investors to benefit from the power of compounding, where the returns earned on an investment are reinvested to generate even more returns over time. This compounding effect can lead to significant wealth accumulation over the long run, making long-term investing a popular strategy for retirement planning or other long-term financial goals.

Long-term investing requires a disciplined and patient approach, as short-term fluctuations in the market can lead to temporary declines in the value of investments. However, over the long run, economic growth and the increasing profitability of well-run companies tend to result in rising stock prices and other forms of investment returns. Long-term investors who can resist the temptation to make short-term trades based on market volatility and focus on investing in high-quality assets can potentially earn substantial returns over time. Moreover, long-term investing can help mitigate some of the risks associated with short-term investing, such as market timing and liquidity risks, by providing a more stable and predictable investment environment for investors. Overall, a long-term investment horizon can be an effective way to build wealth over time and achieve long-term financial goals.

Effective engagement with companies

Effective engagement of investors with their investments is essential for maximizing returns and achieving long-term financial goals. Engaged investors are more likely to make informed decisions about their investments, stay committed to their investment strategies during times of market volatility, and take advantage of opportunities for growth and diversification. Here are some ways to effectively engage investors with their investments:

First, it is essential to provide investors with clear and transparent information about their investments. Investors should have access to up-to-date information about the performance of their investments, including detailed reports on their holdings, investment returns, and fees. This information can help investors make informed decisions about their investments and stay on track with their investment goals.

Second, communication is key to effective investor engagement. Investment managers should regularly communicate with their clients about market trends, investment strategies, and potential risks and opportunities. This communication should be tailored to the individual needs and preferences of each investor, taking into account their risk tolerance, investment goals, and other factors.

Third, investor education is an essential component of effective engagement. Investment managers should provide educational resources to their clients, including webinars, seminars, and other educational materials that can help investors better understand their investments and the broader financial landscape. This education can help investors make more informed investment decisions, stay up-to-date with market trends, and feel more confident in their investment strategies.

Finally, technology can play a significant role in effective investor engagement. Investment managers can leverage technology to provide investors with access to their accounts, investment performance data, and other information in real time. This technology can help investors stay engaged with their investments, monitor their performance, and make informed investment decisions.

Investing in the real economy

The real economy refers to the production and consumption of goods and services in an economy, as opposed to the financial economy, which involves the buying and selling of financial instruments such as stocks, bonds, and derivatives. The real economy encompasses a wide range of industries and sectors, including manufacturing, agriculture, construction, transportation, healthcare, and education.

In the real economy, goods and services are produced by businesses, consumed by households, and traded between countries. Economic growth in the real economy is driven by factors such as technological innovation, productivity gains, and population growth.

FIGURE 2.2 Some additional ideas on how to create long-term value.

Investing in the real economy involves investing in companies that produce goods and services, such as manufacturers, retailers, and service providers. These companies can provide investors with exposure to the real economy and potential long-term growth opportunities.

OTHER WAYS TO CREATE LONG-TERM VALUE

In a way, there are many more ways in which long-term value can be promoted in the company. Figure 2.2 presents some ideas on relevant strategies that can help companies create long-term value while aligning with sustainability ambitions.

By adopting these and other strategies, companies can create long-term value that benefits all stakeholders, including customers, employees, investors, and society as a whole. This also helps promote more sustainable development of such companies, and it can result in a win-win situation for everyone.

GROWING INTEREST AND POSITIVE OUTCOMES

In 2015, Friede, Busch, and Bassen conducted a comprehensive study on the integration of ESG (environmental, social, and governance) factors in investment decision-making. The study showed that there is a significant growing interest in sustainable finance (SF) and that approximately 90% of their results show nonnegative results for the integration of ESG factors in general.

The study analyzed over 2,000 empirical studies from various sources, including academic journals, industry reports, and institutional investors. The findings revealed that the integration of ESG factors in investment decision-making had been steadily increasing over the years, and this trend is expected to continue in the future.

Furthermore, the study found that companies with high ESG performance tend to have better financial performance than those with low ESG performance. The results were consistent across different asset classes and geographies, indicating that ESG factors are relevant for all types of investments.

One of the key drivers of this trend is the increasing awareness of the impact of climate change and other sustainability issues on financial performance. Investors are recognizing the importance of ESG factors in identifying potential risks and opportunities, as well as in contributing to the long-term sustainability of their investments.

The study also highlighted the importance of standardized ESG reporting and disclosure. Without reliable and comparable information on ESG performance, it is difficult for investors to make informed decisions and for companies to demonstrate their commitment to sustainability.

WHY TO DO IT? WHERE THERE IS VALUE AND THERE IS RISK

The study by Battiston, Mandel, Monasterolo, Schütze, and Visentin (2017) is an important contribution to the literature on financial stability and systemic risk. It highlights the need for a more holistic approach to financial regulation that takes into account the complex interconnectivity of the financial system. The study provides a framework for policymakers and regulators to address the challenges posed by systemic risk and to promote the stability of the global financial system. This is a seminal study that examines the complex relationships between financial systems and the real economy. The study highlights the need for a systemic approach to financial stability that takes into account the interconnectivity of financial institutions and the potential for cascading failures.

The authors argue that the traditional approach to financial regulation, which focuses on individual institutions and their risk management practices, is insufficient to address systemic risks. Instead, they propose a framework that considers the entire financial system as a network of interconnected institutions and their relationships.

The study uses network analysis to model the interconnectivity of the global financial system, and it identifies several key characteristics of systemic risk. The authors also identify feedback loops as a source of systemic risk, where shocks to one part of the system can have ripple effects throughout the network. This can lead to cascading failures and a breakdown of the entire system.

Based on their findings, the authors propose a new framework for financial stability that includes three levels of analysis: micro-prudential regulation at the level of individual institutions, meso-prudential regulation at the level of the financial system, and macro-prudential regulation at the level of the economy as a whole.

CHOOSING A VALUATION METHOD

Choosing the right financial valuation method depends on the type of asset being valued, the purpose of the valuation, and the availability and quality of data. Here are some factors to consider when selecting a financial valuation method:

Type of asset: Different valuation methods are more suitable for different types of assets. For example, DCF analysis may be more appropriate for valuing a business, while comparable company analysis may be more suitable for valuing a publicly traded company.

Purpose of valuation: The purpose of the valuation should also be considered when selecting a valuation method. For instance, if the purpose of the valuation is to determine the fair value of an asset for financial reporting purposes, a DCF analysis may be more appropriate than a precedent transaction analysis.

Availability and quality of data: The availability and quality of data can also influence the choice of valuation method. If there is limited data available, a valuation method that relies on a large number of comparable companies or transactions may not be suitable.

Degree of subjectivity: Some valuation methods are more subjective than others. For example, the market approach (using comparable company analysis or precedent transaction analysis) is more subjective than the income approach (using DCF analysis), as it relies on the analyst's judgment and interpretation of the data.

Standards and regulations: Finally, it is important to consider standards and regulations when selecting a valuation method. For example, the International Valuation Standards Council (IVSC) provides guidelines for selecting a valuation method, and regulatory bodies such as the US Securities and Exchange Commission (SEC) may have specific requirements for valuing certain types of assets.

DIFFERENT WAYS TO CREATE VALUE THROUGH SUSTAINABILITY

There are different ways to approach a problem, and that is the case of valuation. Value creation through sustainability is a growing trend among businesses that recognize the potential benefits of integrating sustainability into their operations. One of the key ways that businesses can create value through sustainability is by reducing costs, risks, and waste. By adopting sustainable practices, businesses can minimize their environmental footprint and reduce their reliance on costly resources. Another way to create value is by optimizing product performance through sustainable design and innovation. This can lead to increased efficiency, improved customer satisfaction, and a competitive edge in the market. Innovative strategies to drive revenue growth, such as developing sustainable products and services, can also create value. Finally, businesses can create intangible value by enhancing their corporate culture and brand leadership through their commitment to sustainability, which can improve employee morale and attract socially conscious consumers. Overall, value creation through sustainability has the potential to benefit both the business and the environment, making it an increasingly important consideration for companies looking to succeed in the long term. See Figure 2.3 for more.

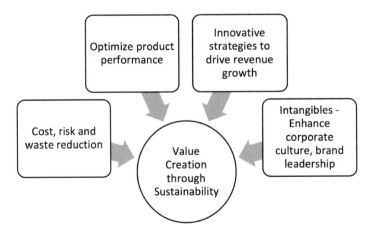

FIGURE 2.3 Value creation through sustainability.

EXAMPLES OF VALUATION METHODS

Hedonic valuation

Hedonic valuation is a method of estimating the value of a good or service by breaking it down into its individual characteristics or attributes and assessing the contribution of each to the overall value. This method is often used in real estate, where the value of a property is determined by analyzing its individual characteristics such as location, size, amenities, and condition.

The hedonic valuation method assumes that the value of a good or service is derived from the utility or satisfaction that it provides to consumers. By analyzing the individual attributes of a good or service, the method can identify which attributes are most important to consumers and how much they are willing to pay for them.

Cost–benefit analysis

Cost-benefit analysis (CBA) is a systematic process used to evaluate the potential costs and benefits of a project or investment decision. It is a method used by businesses, governments, and other organizations to assess the economic feasibility of a proposed project or investment and to compare it with other alternatives.

The process of CBA involves identifying all relevant costs and benefits associated with a project or investment, quantifying them in monetary terms, and comparing them to determine whether the benefits outweigh the costs.

CBA is often used to evaluate public policy decisions, such as infrastructure projects, healthcare interventions, and environmental regulations. It is also commonly used in business settings to assess the potential return on investment for new products, services, or capital investments. CBA is a valuable tool for decision-making because it allows decision-makers to evaluate the potential costs and benefits of a project or investment in a systematic and objective manner and to make informed choices based on a clear understanding of the trade-offs involved.

Other traditional financial methods

Some traditional methods that are common used in finance include time value of money (TVM), DCF, market multiples, and replacement cost. This is not a comprehensive list but rather representative.

TVM is the most popular but is not the only valuation method in finance. There are several other valuation methods that are commonly used in finance, depending on the specific context and type of financial asset being valued. For some of the other common valuation methods see Appendix A.

DCF is a valuation method that estimates the value of an investment based on its future cash flows, discounted back to its present value using a discount rate.

Market multiples use ratios such as price-to-earnings (P/E) or price-to-sales (P/S) to compare the value of a company to its peers or the broader market.

Replacement cost estimates the value of an asset by estimating the cost of replacing it with a similar asset.

IS THERE A GREEN PENALTY?

While there may be some short-term costs or disadvantages associated with adopting sustainable practices, the long-term benefits and competitive advantages are likely to outweigh them. As such, companies should view sustainability as an opportunity for innovation and growth rather than a penalty to be avoided. The term "green penalty" (Gottsman & Kessler, 1998) is used to describe the additional costs or disadvantages that companies may face when adopting environmentally sustainable practices compared to those that do not prioritize environmental concerns. This can include higher upfront costs for eco-friendly materials or equipment, compliance with environmental regulations, and other expenses associated with sustainable operations.

However, the concept of a green penalty is somewhat controversial, as it assumes that environmental sustainability is inherently costly or disadvantageous, which is not always the case. In fact, many studies have found that sustainable practices can lead to cost savings in the long term, as well as other benefits such as improved brand reputation, customer loyalty, and employee satisfaction. Furthermore, as environmental concerns become more pressing and consumers demand more sustainable products and services, companies that fail to prioritize sustainability may face greater costs and disadvantages in the long run. This is because they may be seen as outdated or unresponsive to changing consumer preferences and may face reputational damage or regulatory penalties for failing to meet environmental standards.

MATERIALITY

Materiality in finance refers to the concept that certain financial information is considered material or important if its omission or misstatement could influence the decisions of investors, creditors, or other stakeholders. Materiality is a key concept in financial reporting and auditing, as it helps determine what information should be disclosed in financial statements and other financial reports.

The materiality threshold is determined by a variety of factors, including the nature and magnitude of the financial information, the characteristics of the users of the financial statements, and the overall context of the financial reporting. For example, an error in financial reporting that is relatively small in magnitude may still be considered material if it affects a key metric, such as earnings per share or net income, and has the potential to impact the decisions of investors or other stakeholders.

The materiality threshold is typically determined by professional standards and guidelines, such as the Generally Accepted Accounting Principles (GAAP) or International Financial Reporting Standards (IFRS). These standards provide guidance on how to determine whether certain financial information is material and require companies and auditors to disclose any material information that could impact the decisions of investors, creditors, or other stakeholders.

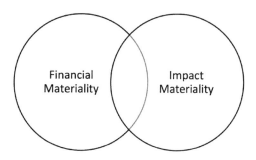

FIGURE 2.4 Double materiality.

DOUBLE MATERIALITY

Double materiality recognizes the importance of both financial and non-financial factors in evaluating a company's performance and impact on stakeholders. Double materiality is a concept used in sustainability reporting that recognizes the impact of both financial and non-financial factors on a company's performance. The term "double materiality" refers to the idea that a company's actions can have both financial and non-financial impacts that are material to different stakeholders (Adams et al., 2021; Baumüller & Sopp, 2022).

From a financial perspective, a company's performance is typically evaluated based on its financial statements and reports, such as its income statement, balance sheet, and cash flow statement. These financial metrics provide information on the company's revenue, expenses, profits, and cash flows. However, from a non-financial perspective, a company's performance is also evaluated based on its impact on ESG factors. This includes factors such as carbon emissions, human rights practices, labor standards, and corporate governance. In the context of double materiality, a company's financial performance can be impacted by its non-financial performance and vice versa. For example, a company with poor labor standards may face reputational damage, which could impact its financial performance. Similarly, a company with high carbon emissions may face regulatory risks, which could also impact its financial performance. A double materiality representation can be seen in Figure 2.4.

TRAILBLAZING RESEARCH
ADVANCING LONG-TERM VALUE CREATION

In the realm of Long-Term Value Creation for Sustainable Finance, thrree are many influential authors. Among them we find: Mazzucato, Raworth, and Edmans (in no particular order), who have emerged to set path on groundbreaking research. Through their respective work, they have pushed the boundaries of economic and financial theory and offered fresh perspectives on how to achieve sustainable and inclusive growth. Their original work has fostered a paradigm shift in understanding the interplay between finance, value creation, and societal well-being.

Mariana Mazzucato, in her book "The Value of Everything: Making and Taking in the Global Economy," (Mazzucato, 2018) critically examines prevailing notions of value and their impact on the global economy. By emphasizing the need to redefine value to encompass environmental and social dimensions, Mazzucato's work lays a foundation for a more holistic approach to sustainable finance.

Kate Raworth's book, "Doughnut Economics: Seven Ways to Think Like a 21st-Century Economist," (Raworth, 2017) presents a transformative economic model. This model promotes the concept of "doughnut economics," which seeks to balance the essential needs of humanity within planetary boundaries. Raworth's pioneering ideas challenge traditional economic thinking and provide a framework for long-term value creation that integrates social and environmental considerations.

Alex Edmans, in "Grow the Pie: How Great Companies Deliver Both Purpose and Profit," (Edmans, 2021) explores the correlation between purpose and profit in the business world. By showcasing exemplary companies that prioritize both financial success and broader social objectives, Edmans demonstrates that sustainable value creation can be achieved through a purpose-driven approach. His insights shed light on the importance of aligning corporate goals with societal and environmental well-being.

IN A NUTSHELL

Financial valuation is a crucial aspect of investment decision-making, and it requires a thorough understanding of financial concepts, market conditions, and valuation methods. The accuracy of a valuation depends on the quality of the data and assumptions used in the analysis, as well as the experience and expertise of the analyst conducting the valuation. Ultimately, financial valuation is not an exact science, and it involves a degree of subjectivity and judgment. However, by using a rigorous and disciplined approach, investors and financial analysts can increase their chances of making sound investment decisions and achieving their financial goals.

DISCUSSION QUESTIONS

1   Why is financial valuation important?
2   What are some commonly used methods for financial valuation?
3   What is the difference between tangible and intangible value?
4   How can companies create long-term value?
5   How can investors engage effectively with their investments?
6   What are some factors to consider when selecting a financial valuation method?
7   What are some common valuation methods used in finance?
8   What is the market approach in financial valuation?
9   What is important in determining the right financial valuation method?
10 Why is materiality an important concept in finance?

WORKS CITED

Adams, C. A., Alhamood, A., He, X., Tian, J., Wang, L., & Wang, Y. (2021). *The double-materiality concept: Application and issues*. Global Reporting Initiative (GRI).

Battiston, S., Mandel, A., Monasterolo, I., Schütze, F., & Visentin, G. (2017). A climate stress-test of the financial system. *Nature Climate Change, 7*(4), 283–288.

Baumüller, J., & Sopp, K. (2022). Double materiality and the shift from non-financial to European sustainability reporting: Review, outlook and implications. *Journal of Applied Accounting Research, 23*(1), 8–28.

Dallas, L. L. (2011). Short-termism, the financial crisis, and corporate governance. *Journal of Corporation Law, 37*, 264.

Edmans, A. (2021). *Grow the pie: How great companies deliver both purpose and profit–updated and revised*. Cambridge University Press.

Eisfeldt, A. L., Kim, E., & Papanikolaou, D. (2020). Intangible value. *Working paper 28056*. National Bureau of Economic Research.

Friede, G., Busch, T., & Bassen, A. (2015). ESG and financial performance: aggregated evidence from more than 2000 empirical studies. *Journal of Sustainable Finance & Investment, 5*(4), 210–233.

Gottsman, L., & Kessler, J. (1998). Smart screened investments: Environmentally screened equity funds that perform like conventional funds. *The Journal of Investing, 7*(3), 15–24.

Koller, T., Goedhart, M., & Wessels, D. (2010). *Valuation: Measuring and managing the value of companies* (Vol. 499). John Wiley and Sons.

Marginson, D., & McAulay, L. (2008). Exploring the debate on short-termism: A theoretical and empirical analysis. *Strategic Management Journal, 29*(3), 273–292.

Mazzucato, M. (2018). *The value of everything: Making and taking in the global economy*. Hachette UK.

Raworth, K. (2017). *Doughnut economics: Seven ways to think like a 21st-century economist*. Chelsea Green Publishing.

CHAPTER 3

Financial institutions

THERE ARE BANKS, AND THERE ARE BANKS

We typically have these two categories for banks, depending on the kind of business they do: commercial banks and investment banks. Commercial banks are those that we all know well. The ones that have branches in shopping centers and the main street (Harjoto, Mullineaux, & Yi, 2006). Those are the kinds of banks that typically accept deposits and provide loans, mortgages, lending, credit cards, and several other things. And we also have another category, which is investment banks. They underwrite financial products, and they act as intermediaries between issuers and investors with securities. In the case of the United States, the distinction between commercial and investment banks was very clear until 1999.

WHAT IS SUSTAINABLE BANKING?

Sustainable banking (Weber & Feltmate, 2016) is a type of banking that aims to integrate environmental, social, and governance (ESG) criteria into financial decision-making. Sustainable banking usually promotes and deploys different activities within SF, i.e., sustainable asset management, which can be relevant for the management of their client's investment portfolios.

Although sustainable banking can encompass a wide range of products and activities, some of their key services include sustainability assessments and ratings and ESG data services across different companies and sectors.

A LITTLE BIT OF HISTORY

Regulators kept those the functions of commercial and investment banks separated and prevented some complications by establishing precise limits on what certain banks could do. For example, it was also difficult for banks to cross state lines because they could not go beyond certain geographical boundaries to limit their scope. But also, financial activities permitted by certain financial institutions were heavily regulated before the repeal of the Glass Steagall Act. This act that prevented securities' firms and investment banks from taking deposits, among other things, was passed in 1933 and repealed in 1999.

DOI: 10.4324/9781003274735-3

And there is a rationale for keeping both of those functions separated. As commercial banks deal with savings and have direct contact with individual clients, investment banks deal with more sophisticated and complex approaches. And those two activities, in a way, represent very distinct risk profiles for such activities.

But did the repeal of the Glass Steagall Act cause the financial crisis? In the opinion of some experts, the answer might be yes (Crawford, 2011; Sakbani, 2009).

TOO BIG-TO-FAIL COMPANIES

"Too big to fail" (TBTF) (Stern & Feldman, 2004) are those considered so large and interconnected with the wider economy that their failure could have catastrophic consequences for the economy as a whole. In other words, these corporations are deemed "systemically important" due to their size, complexity, and significance to the functioning of the financial system. During a financial crisis, the failure of a TBTF corporation could trigger a chain reaction of bankruptcies and defaults, leading to a collapse of the financial system and a severe economic downturn. This is why governments and central banks often step in to bail out TBTF corporations in order to prevent such a scenario.

TBTF corporations are typically large banks, insurance companies, or other financial institutions, although they can also be companies in other industries that are considered critical to the functioning of the economy. The concept of TBTF corporations has been controversial, as some argue that it creates a moral hazard by incentivizing these companies to take excessive risks, knowing that they will be bailed out if they fail. However, others argue that allowing these companies to fail could have even more severe consequences for the wider economy and that a better solution would be to regulate these companies more strictly to prevent excessive risk-taking in the first place.

Lehman Brothers – the failure of the financial system

The bankruptcy of Lehman Brothers in September 2008 is widely considered to be a key event that triggered the financial crisis of 2008–2009. Lehman Brothers was a large investment bank and one of the biggest players in the market for mortgage-backed securities, which were at the heart of the crisis (Adu-Gyamfi, 2016). When the housing market collapsed, and many homeowners defaulted on their mortgages, the value of the mortgage-backed securities held by Lehman Brothers and other financial institutions plummeted. This created a chain reaction of losses and write-downs, which ultimately led to the collapse of Lehman Brothers.

The bankruptcy of Lehman Brothers sent shockwaves through the financial system, as it was a major counterparty to many other financial institutions and had significant exposure to other parts of the financial system. The collapse of Lehman Brothers caused a crisis of confidence in the financial system, as investors and creditors became worried about the solvency of other financial institutions. This led to a freezing of credit markets, as banks and other financial institutions became reluctant to lend to each other for fear of counterparty risk. This, in turn, led to a credit crunch that made it difficult for businesses and households to access credit, which contributed to the broader economic downturn. The bankruptcy of Lehman Brothers is therefore seen as a key event in the financial crisis, as it exposed the fragility of the financial system and triggered a chain reaction of losses and write-downs that ultimately led to a broader economic downturn.

SF REGULATION

Regulations in this field aim to encourage financial institutions to consider ESG factors when making investment decisions. Such regulations vary around the world, but some notable examples include the following:

Europe: In 2019, the European Union (EU) introduced an SF taxonomy, which provides a standardized classification system for sustainable economic activities. The EU also requires asset managers to disclose how they integrate ESG factors into their investment decisions.

United States: The US Securities and Exchange Commission (SEC) has recently stepped up its focus on ESG disclosures and is considering implementing a rule that would require public companies to disclose their ESG risks and opportunities.

China: In 2020, China introduced guidelines for green bonds, which are used to finance environmentally friendly projects. The guidelines set out criteria for what qualifies as a green project and require issuers to disclose how the funds will be used.

Japan: In 2020, Japan's Ministry of Environment released guidelines for green finance, which include requirements for financial institutions to disclose how they are integrating ESG factors into their investment decisions.

Australia: The Australian Securities and Investments Commission (ASIC) has released guidance for companies on how to disclose their climate-related risks and opportunities. The guidance also includes recommendations on how to integrate climate risk into a company's overall risk management framework.

Overall, the trend toward SF regulations is growing globally, with more countries introducing rules and guidelines to encourage ESG integration into financial decision-making.

FIDUCIARY RESPONSIBILITY

Fiduciary responsibility refers to the legal and ethical obligation of a person or entity to act in the best interests of another party. A fiduciary is someone who has been entrusted with the responsibility to act on behalf of another person or organization and is required to put the interests of that party ahead of their own. Fiduciary responsibility can be easily summarized in one simple idea, "act in the best interest of clients."

Fiduciary responsibility is often associated with financial or legal matters, such as a trustee managing a trust on behalf of a beneficiary or an investment advisor managing a client's assets. In these situations, the fiduciary is legally obligated to act in the best interests of their client or beneficiary and must avoid any conflicts of interest that could compromise their duty of loyalty and care. Fiduciary responsibility requires the fiduciary to exercise prudence, diligence, and loyalty in their actions and decisions and to always act in good faith and with the best interests of their client or beneficiary in mind. Any breach of fiduciary responsibility can result in legal or financial penalties and can damage the fiduciary's reputation and credibility.

CREATING SUSTAINABLE VALUE THROUGH BANKING INTERMEDIATION

Banks can create sustainable value through banking intermediation by prioritizing sustainable investments and initiatives in their decision-making processes and by providing sustainable banking products and services to customers. By doing so, banks can contribute to the transition to a more sustainable economy and promote sustainable development.

Deposits

Banks can create sustainable value through deposits by offering sustainable banking products and services that incentivize customers to deposit their money with the bank. This can include offering higher interest rates for sustainable investments or green deposits and providing transparency about how customer deposits are used to fund sustainable initiatives.

Credit and lending

Banks can create sustainable value through credit and lending by prioritizing sustainable investments and projects in their lending decisions. This can include providing loans for renewable energy projects, sustainable agriculture, and green infrastructure. Banks can also offer lower interest rates for sustainable investments and penalize unsustainable investments.

Green mortgages

Banks can create sustainable value through green mortgages by providing lower interest rates for mortgages on energy-efficient homes, green buildings, and sustainable housing projects. This incentivizes customers to invest in sustainable homes and contributes to reducing carbon emissions.

Investment banking and VC

Banks can create sustainable value through investment banking and venture capital activities by prioritizing sustainable investments in their portfolio. This can include investing in renewable energy, sustainable agriculture, and green technologies. Banks can also work with startups to develop sustainable business models and offer advisory services to help these companies grow sustainably.

Underwriting financial products

Banks can create sustainable value through underwriting financial products by prioritizing sustainable investments in their underwriting decisions. This can include underwriting sustainable bonds, green funds, and other sustainable financial products that promote sustainable investments.

Consultancy and advisory role

Banks can create sustainable value through consultancy and advisory services by providing advice and guidance to businesses and individuals on how to incorporate sustainability into their operations and investment decisions. This can include providing sustainability assessments, advising on sustainable investments, and helping businesses to develop sustainable business models. Banks can act as consultants to small and medium-sized companies. Banks have a wealth of financial expertise and experience that they can offer to their customers, including advice on cash flow management, financial planning, risk management, and access to capital.

BEYOND THE BANKING HORIZON

Other banking activities beyond the traditional banking arena can also be relevant, i.e., crowdfunding or microfinance.

Crowdfunding

Crowdfunding is a way of raising funds for a project or business venture by soliciting small contributions from a large number of people, typically via the internet. Crowdfunding platforms allow individuals or businesses to create a fundraising campaign and invite people to contribute money in exchange for a reward, such as a product or service, or simply as a donation (Belleflamme, Omrani, & Peitz, 2015).

There are several types of crowdfunding, including:

Donation-based crowdfunding: This type of crowdfunding is used by non-profit organizations or social causes to raise money from donors who believe in the cause and want to support it.

Rewards-based crowdfunding: This type of crowdfunding is used by entrepreneurs or small businesses to raise money by offering rewards or perks to those who contribute. The rewards can range from products or services to exclusive access or experiences.

Equity-based crowdfunding: This type of crowdfunding allows investors to buy shares of a company in exchange for their investment. This is similar to traditional venture capital funding but allows smaller investors to participate.

Debt-based crowdfunding: This type of crowdfunding allows businesses to raise money by borrowing from a large number of investors, who are repaid with interest over time.

Crowdfunding can be a useful way for entrepreneurs, artists, and social causes to raise funds without the need for traditional financing or investment. However, it can also be challenging to stand out among the many crowdfunding campaigns competing for attention, and success often depends on a strong marketing and social media strategy, as well as a compelling message and rewards for contributors.

Microfinance

Microcredit, also known as microfinance, is a type of financial service that provides small loans, savings accounts, and other financial products to low-income individuals and communities who lack access to traditional banking services. Microcredit is typically provided by specialized microfinance institutions or non-profit organizations and is designed to help lift people out of poverty and promote economic development (Mahmud, 2003).

The loans provided through microcredit are often very small, ranging from just a few dollars to a few thousand dollars, and are usually used for small business ventures, such as starting a small farm or shop, purchasing equipment, or investing in education or training. The loans are typically repaid over a period of several months to a few years and often have higher interest rates than traditional bank loans to offset the risks involved in lending to individuals without a credit history or collateral.

Microcredit has been successful in many parts of the world, particularly in developing countries, where traditional banking services may be unavailable or unaffordable for low-income individuals. By providing access to credit and financial services, microcredit programs can help individuals start or grow small businesses, increase their incomes, and improve their standard of living. Microcredit programs have also faced criticism for their high interest rates and for the potential for borrowers to become trapped in a cycle of debt. To address these concerns, some microfinance institutions have introduced measures such as financial education and counseling to help borrowers manage their loans and build financial literacy skills.

IMPACT INVESTING

Impact investing is a type of investment approach that seeks to generate both financial returns and positive social or environmental impact. Impact investors are individuals or organizations who seek to invest in companies or projects that have the potential to address social or environmental challenges while generating a financial return on their investment.

The goal of impact investing is to create positive social or environmental change through market-based solutions rather than relying solely on traditional philanthropy or government aid. Impact investors typically invest in companies or projects that have a social or environmental mission, such as renewable energy, affordable housing, or sustainable agriculture. They may also seek to invest in companies that have strong social or environmental practices, such as fair labor standards or environmentally responsible supply chains.

Impact investing has become increasingly popular in recent years as more investors seek to align their investments with their values and make a positive impact on the world. Impact investors may invest through various types of vehicles, including mutual funds, exchange traded funds, and private equity or venture capital funds. The big challenge of impact investing is measuring the social or environmental impact of investments, as well as balancing the financial returns with the social or environmental goals. However, impact investors and organizations are working to develop standardized metrics and tools for measuring impact in order to make impact investing more transparent and effective.

FIGURE 3.1 Typical sectors for sustainable banking.

SECTORS FOR SUSTAINABLE BANKING

The traditional sectors of sustainable banking encompass a wide range of industries and sectors, as can be observed in Figure 3.1, including agriculture, arts and culture, energy, lending, healthcare, community development, education, and others. These sectors are characterized by their significant impact on society and the environment, and banks have a critical role to play in promoting sustainable development within these sectors.

In the agriculture sector, sustainable banking can support sustainable farming practices, such as organic farming, regenerative agriculture, and sustainable land use. This can include providing financing for sustainable farming projects, offering crop insurance, and providing advice and guidance on sustainable farming practices.

In the arts and culture sector, sustainable banking can support sustainable cultural initiatives and creative projects that promote social and environmental sustainability. This can include providing financing for sustainable cultural projects, supporting sustainable tourism initiatives, and promoting sustainable practices in the arts and culture industry.

In the energy sector, sustainable banking can support the transition to renewable energy sources and energy efficiency. This can include providing financing for renewable energy projects, such as solar and wind power, and offering financial incentives for energy-efficient technologies and practices.

In the lending sector, sustainable banking can prioritize sustainable investments and projects in lending decisions. This can include offering lower interest rates for sustainable investments, penalizing unsustainable investments, and providing advice and guidance on sustainable investment strategies.

In the healthcare sector, sustainable banking can support sustainable healthcare practices and initiatives that promote social and environmental sustainability. This can include providing financing for sustainable healthcare projects, promoting sustainable healthcare practices, and supporting research and development of sustainable healthcare technologies.

In the community development sector, sustainable banking can support sustainable community development initiatives, such as affordable housing, community infrastructure, and sustainable transportation. This can include providing financing for sustainable community development projects, offering financial incentives for sustainable transportation, and supporting sustainable urban planning initiatives.

In the education sector, sustainable banking can support sustainable education initiatives and sustainable development education. This can include providing financing for sustainable education projects, promoting sustainable education practices, and supporting research and development of sustainable education technologies.

In addition to these traditional sectors, sustainable banking can also support a wide range of other sectors and industries, i.e., technology, manufacturing, and finance. By promoting sustainable development across all sectors, banks can play a critical role in the transition to a more sustainable economy and contribute to a more just and equitable society.

PRINCIPLES OF RESPONSIBLE BANKING[1]

The Principles of Responsible Banking (UNEP, 2022) were launched in 2019 by the United Nations Environment Programme Finance Initiative (UNEP FI) in collaboration with 130 banks from around the world. The principles represent a framework for banks to align their strategies and operations with the United Nations' Sustainable Development Goals (SDGs) (United Nations, 2022) and the Paris Agreement on Climate Change.

The Principles of Responsible Banking, as seen in Figure 3.2, provide a framework for banks to transition toward a more sustainable business model by committing to integrating sustainability into their core business practices. This includes shifting their lending portfolios toward sustainable investments, setting sustainability targets and measuring impact, engaging with stakeholders, and promoting sustainable practices throughout the financial system. By aligning their business activities with the SDGs and the Paris Agreement on Climate Change, banks can play a critical role in advancing sustainable development and contributing to a more just and equitable society.

FIGURE 3.2 The six Principles of Responsible Banking (UNEP, 2022).

WHY IS THIS IMPORTANT?

For banks, their most relevant impact is on what they finance. The report "Banking on Climate Chaos 2022"[2] (Rainforest Action Network et al., 2022) by the advocacy group Oil Change International provides a detailed analysis of the role that the world's largest banks play in financing the fossil fuel industry and contributing to climate change. The report argues that despite increasing rhetoric about commitments to sustainability and the Paris Agreement, many of the largest banks are continuing to finance fossil fuel projects at a significant scale.

The report highlights the fact that the top banks around the world have provided over US$3.8 trillion in financing to the fossil fuel industry since the Paris Agreement was signed in 2015. This financing includes both direct funding for fossil fuel projects and investments in companies that are heavily involved in the industry. The report also identifies the top 20 banks that are the worst offenders in terms of financing fossil fuels, with several US banks topping the list. The report argues that the continued financing of the fossil fuel industry by major banks is contributing to climate change and undermining efforts to meet the goals of the Paris Agreement. The report also highlights the significant environmental and social impacts of fossil fuel projects, including damage to local ecosystems, displacement of indigenous communities, and air and water pollution. The report concludes with a call to action for banks to end their financing of the fossil fuel industry and instead prioritize investments in renewable energy and other sustainable projects. The report argues that this shift is necessary in order to address the urgent global challenge of climate change and to create a more sustainable and just economy.

Reports like this are more and more relevant to stakeholders, and this is not even the only one showing how more in-depth analysis can be done on the accountability of banks and the composition of their lending portfolios[3] (CERES Accelerator for Sustainable Capital Markets, 2022).

IN A NUTSHELL

Sustainability is important in banking for several reasons. Banks have a significant impact on the environment, and promoting sustainability can help reduce negative impacts and promote sustainable practices. Banks also have a social responsibility to address global challenges like climate change and poverty. Sustainability is critical for economic stability, and banks can play a crucial role by financing sustainable businesses and technologies. Customers are increasingly demanding sustainable banking options, and banks that fail to meet these demands risk losing customers. Additionally, many governments have implemented regulations promoting sustainability, and banks that fail to comply may face financial and legal penalties.

DISCUSSION QUESTIONS

1   What are the main differences between commercial and investment banks?
2   What is the rationale for separating commercial and investment banking activities?
3   What is the Glass Steagall Act, and when was it repealed?

4   Did the repeal of the Glass Steagall Act cause the financial crisis? Why?
5   What is fiduciary responsibility?
6   How can banks create sustainable value through banking intermediation?
7   What kind of services can banks offer to small and medium-sized companies?
8   What is crowdfunding, and what are the different types of crowdfunding?
9   How can crowdfunding be useful for entrepreneurs and social causes?
10 What is microfinance, and how does it work?

NOTES

1   For further reference, see https://www.unepfi.org/banking/bankingprinciples/
2   For further reference, see the complete report: https://priceofoil.org/content/uploads/2022/03/Banking-on-Climate-Chaos-2022.pdf
3   For further reference, see another report: https://www.ceres.org/resources/reports/derivatives-bank-climate-risk

WORKS CITED

Adu-Gyamfi, M. (2016). The bankruptcy of lehman brothers: Causes, effects and lessons learnt. *Journal of insurance and financial Management, 1*(4), 132–149.

Belleflamme, P., Omrani, N., & Peitz, M. (2015). The economics of crowdfunding platforms. *Information Economics and Policy, 33*, 11–28.

CERES Accelerator for Sustainable Capital Markets. (2022). *Derivatives & Bank Climate Risk Financing a Net Zero Economy.* CERES.

Crawford, C. (2011). The repeal of the Glass-Steagall Act and the current financial crisis. *Journal of Business & Economics Research (JBER), 9*(1). https://doi.org/10.19030/jber.v9i1.949

Harjoto, M., Mullineaux, D. J., & Yi, H. C. (2006). A comparison of syndicated loan pricing at investment and commercial banks. *Financial Management, 35*(4), 49–70.

Mahmud, S. (2003). Actually how empowering is microcredit? *Development and Change, 344*(4), 577–605.

Rainforest Action Alliance, Banktrack, Indigenous Environmental Network, Oilchange International, Reclaim Finance, Sierra Club, & Urgewald. (2022). *Banking on Climate Chaos: Fossil Fuel Finance Report 2022.* BankingonClimateChaos.org.

Sakbani, M. (2009). The global financial crisis, central banking and the reform of the international monetary and financial system. In Hieronymi, O. (Ed.), *Globalization and the Reform of the International Banking and Monetary System* (pp. 104–129). London: Palgrave Macmillan.

Stern, G. H., & Feldman, R. J. (2004). *Too big to fail: The hazards of bank bailouts.* Washington, DC: Brookings Institution Press.

UNEP. (2022, March 8). *Principles for Responsible Banking.* Retrieved from: https://www.unepfi.org/banking/bankingprinciples/

United Nations. (2022). *Department of Economic and Social Affairs.* Retrieved from THE 17 GOALS: https://sdgs.un.org/goals

Weber, O., & Feltmate, B. (2016). *Sustainable banking: Managing the social and environmental impact of financial institutions.* Toronto, Ontario: University of Toronto Press.

CHAPTER 4

Different approaches to sustainable finance

DIFFERENT APPROACHES FOR SUSTAINABLE FINANCE

According to *The Economist*, "Environmental, social and governance issues are now a major factor in investment" (K. K., 2018). And this comes to a great extent from the fact that investors evaluated their performance using mostly financial metrics. Environmental, social, and governance (ESG) issues have become relevant criteria for financial valuation, and their relevance is today in the billions and can even reach trillions for some categories.

Sustainable finance (SF) can also take different shapes and forms, i.e., grants, investment, funding, credit, equity, etc. But it can also go by many names (Nicholls, n.d.): venture philanthropy, mission-related investment, development finance, ethical finance, impact finance, green finance, and so on. It is not easy to navigate the terminology, especially for newcomers, but a major part of the very first step to understanding where SF falls is to grasp the so-called spectrum of SF, which we can observe in Figure 4.1.

Figure 4.1 is a stylized representation of what is known as the SF spectrum. There, we can see how different approaches to SF fall between traditional finance and philanthropy. In a way, SF is neither traditional finance nor philanthropy. It aims to maximize both impact and return. Interesting work regarding the SF spectrum can be found in the work of different authors (Kumar Deshpande, 2021; Kumar, Sharma, Rao, Lim, & Mangla, 2022; Valliammal & Manivannan, 2022 are just some examples). Furthermore, this topic can be found in the Handbook of Sustainable Investments[1] by Swiss Sustainable Finance (SSF) and the CFA Research Foundation, part of the CFA Institute.[2] We still do not have enough regulations to agree on the taxonomy of ESG factors. ESG factors are sometimes defined in the way they overlap or even contradict, given the complexity of elements that are included in their assessment, and this can be challenging to classify. ESG factors are in constant evolution and continue to advance and expand even now.

IMPACT INVESTING

Impact refers to what the company does or does not do, i.e., the products and services that they offer and how that value offer or strategy has an effect in the environmental or social dimension. That said, the impact can ideally be positive, but it can also be negative. Impact does not

DOI: 10.4324/9781003274735-4

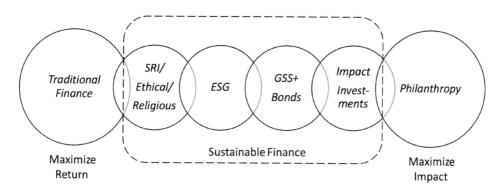

FIGURE 4.1 The SF spectrum.

necessarily fit the measurement criteria of ESG factors, as it is not a standard metric, and so companies that perform highly on ESG can sometimes have a low impact, and vice versa. Both criteria are different. "ESG impact is hard to measure, but it is not impossible" (Howard-Grenville, 2021).

We have mentioned how there are many names for SF, and impact finance or impact investments can often be used as substitutes for SF while they are actually a subset of SF. Impact investment is a term coined circa 2007 in the realm of philanthropy, and some early adopters included Judith Rodin, President of the Rockefeller Foundation, in her book *The Power of Impact Investing: Putting Markets to Work for Profit and Global Good* (Rodin & Brandenburg, 2014).

Impact is an investment strategy that aims to create a positive social and/or environmental impact while aiming to create financial returns. This part is actually when it gets tricky, as impact investment is technically not philanthropy, and it should try to generate at least some financial returns. Some impact investments or financial products put their financial intention as a priority and also aim to achieve impact, while others set their priorities in reverse. As described by Judith Rodin, "Impact investing can be a powerful instrument of change" (Rodin & Brandenburg, 2014).

Is intentionality necessary?

When investing for impact, it is important that the impact be intentional (Hockerts, Hehenberger, Schaltegger, & Farber, 2022). Impact needs to be measured as other metrics, and it is important that it gets reported. Earlier efforts in this area were more niche. However, impact investments today cover a wide range of assets and strategies. We are very far today from the days when impact was the only priority and return was not even necessary. That is how philanthropy started to make inroads into SF, but today those funds are not even that common.

> Impact investments are investments made with the intention to generate positive, measurable social and environmental impact alongside a financial return. Impact investments can be made in both emerging and developed markets and target a range of returns from below market to market rate, depending on investors' strategic goals.
>
> (Global Impact Investment Network, n.d.)

According to the Global Impact Investment Network (GIIN), there are four characteristics or key elements of impact investments: (1) intentionality, (2) investment with return expectations, (3) range of return expectations and asset classes, and (4) impact measurement (Global Impact Investing Network, 2019).

More complex implementations of impact investments have been coined recently. One great example of innovation in impact investments is venture philanthropy, which can be found in Chapter 13.

THEMATIC INVESTING

Thematic investing is also not a novelty in finance. The first thematic fund is believed to be designed in the post-World War II era (Charles Schwab, 2023). Mutual funds and exchange traded funds (ETFs) deploy this technique to cater investment alternatives for their clients to meet specific needs or mandates. By this technique, we choose assets based on a theme or topic of interest, according to the best interest of the client, to provide an appropriate risk and return mix that aligns with the stated theme or topic. "Thematic investments target ideas, personal values, or trends that don't fit squarely into existing industry classifications" (Charles Schwab, 2023).

Some of the above-mentioned topics are also aligned with what the World Economic Forum (WEF) described as the "biggest short- and long-term risks" (World Economic Forum, n.d.) in 2023. We cannot continue to deny the scope of the problems that arise from sustainability in the world we live in. Here is the list of global risks ranked by severity over the short term (two years) and long term (ten years) according to the WEF. Figure 4.3 summarizes some risks that we face globally and that require important investment in the short and the long term.

For big financial institutions like Blackrock,[3] thematic investments can come from megatrends, i.e., rapid urbanization, climate change, resource scarcity, shifting economic power, and demographic and social change, which is, in a way, connected to technological breakthrough (Blackrock, 2023), which again is not that far from those global risks identified by the WEF.

ESG INTEGRATION

ESG integration refers to companies in an industry. A lot of those companies are listed in the stock market, but we can also find interesting implementations for private companies. It is about the issues in a company's operations that end up influencing financial performance. Issues that are material to that company. These issues are identified, measured, and categorized into ESG factors.

> ESG investing grew out of investment philosophies such as Socially Responsible Investing (SRI), but there are key differences. Earlier models typically use value judgments and negative screening to decide which companies to invest in. ESG investing and analysis, on the other hand, looks at finding value in companies – not just at supporting a set of values.
> (CFA Institute, 2023)

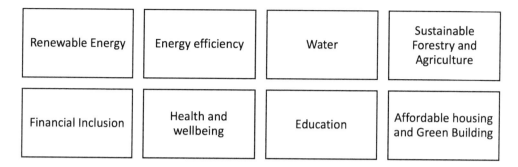

FIGURE 4.2 Examples of thematic investment.

Short term	Long term
1. Cost-of-living crisis	1. Failure to mitigate climate change
2. Natural disasters and extreme weather events	2. Failure of climate change adaption
3. Geoeconomic confrontation	3. Natural disasters and extreme weather events
4. Failure to mitigate climate change	4. Biodiversity loss and ecosystem collapse
5. Erosion of social cohesion and societal polarization	5. Large-scale involuntary migration
6. Large-scale environmental damage incidents	6. Natural resource crises
7. Failure of climate change adaption	7. Erosion of social cohesion and societal polarization
8. Widespread cybercrime and cyber insecurity	8. Widespread cybercrime and cyber insecurity
9. Natural resource crises	9. Geoeconomic confrontation
10. Large-scale involuntary migration	10. Large-scale environmental damage incidents

FIGURE 4.3 Global risks are ranked by severity according to the World Economic Forum (n.d.).

As we can observe in Figure 4.4, there are different styles to engage in ESG integration that come from the basic ESG screening to the more sophisticated and complex impact investment described above.

ESG screening

ESG screening is the most basic style, as it only requires a basic analysis of ESG factors to be able to identify the characteristic of such ESG factors for analysis. ESG screening can involve the exclusion of specific assets, companies, industries, or geographies from an investment portfolio based on ESG risk factors. ESG screening can be applied to portfolios as a standalone approach or in combination with other styles (State Street Global Advisors, 2022).

ESG design

ESG design is a further step of ESG integration, where ESG factors are also used as decision-makers that are weighted into the analysis to choose the best assets for the portfolio. It does

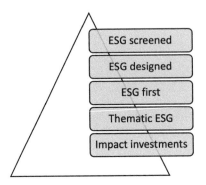

FIGURE 4.4 Different strategies of ESG integration.

require further work and information to work with in order to align it to the investor mandate by establishing more involved goals.

ESG first

ESG first overweights ESG factors in the analysis by establishing a mandate that privileges ESG performance on the design of the portfolio rather than return. This can be aligned to better risk assessment of the chosen portfolio, but not necessarily, as the priority of this style is to optimize the ESG performance of the portfolio.

Thematic ESG

Thematic investments, as the name suggests, seek to establish themes or goals for your design. Some examples of themes can be investments in water, biodiversity, job creation, and combating poverty, but the list can be as long as there are issues. This type of strategy has become very relevant in recent years, especially due to the advancement of technology that allows greater analysis of alternatives and elements in making investment decisions, and some good examples of this can be found in some investment funds that seek to align with specific thematic objectives. In the same way, this is one of those strategies that can be implemented in a good way in conjunction with others.

Impact investment

And if we talk about ESG, we cannot leave impact investments aside. However, we have already defined this term.

STAGES FOR ESG INTEGRATION

ESG factors can be integrated throughout the financial analysis and require a comprehensive and diligent analysis that includes quantitative and qualitative analysis to ultimately promote active ownership. According to Principles of Responsible Investment (PRI)[4], there are four different stages of ESG integration, as can be seen in Figure 4.5.

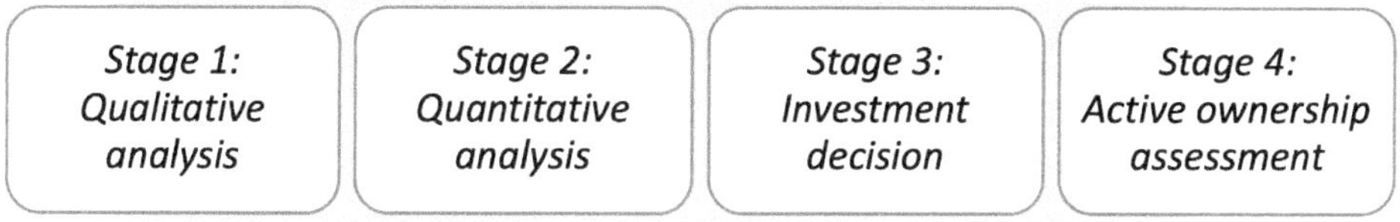

Stage 1: Qualitative analysis	Stage 2: Quantitative analysis	Stage 3: Investment decision	Stage 4: Active ownership assessment

FIGURE 4.5 ESG integration techniques (PRI).

The investment process involves four stages: qualitative analysis, quantitative analysis, investment decision, and active ownership assessment. Investors gather relevant information about a company, assess the impact of financial factors in stages 1 and 2, and make investment decisions, to finally use the outcomes to inform future investment analysis and to actively own their portfolio.

What is the difference between ESG integration and impact?

The line between these two is not always evident, and so perhaps the best way to clarify their difference is by using some examples. We can take an industrial company that ranks high on a number of ESG factors, i.e., health and safety or governance, but might have significantly high emissions. Overall, the ESG rating for said company can be good or even remarkable, but we have to account for negative externalities in this case as well. We can also consider, as an example, a consulting company that helps hundreds of NGOs and social enterprises thrive in their markets. This particular consulting company might have a significant impact, a very positive impact, in fact. However, this might not be reflected by their ESG ratings as they could have a poor track record on certain ESG factors that might not be properly evaluating their line of business, i.e., their choice of location for corporate offices or their use of electricity and water in their facilities. In fact, this is a bit contradictory even, as such a consulting company could really do more to try to incorporate everything that is possible to prove their worth, and it would eventually pay back for them. Any of those two examples can show the concept of impact and make a case for how impact and ESG criteria are not always aligned.

There are many other examples of controversial or contradictory economic activities, i.e., energy and, on top of it, oil and gas. In every activity, and particularly for those that are more complex, we need to assess them. We cannot just flip the switch and have all energy come from renewables over a day. We need to transition to clean energy, but it will take time and money, as explained in Chapter 12. In any case, we need to be practical and realistic about it, and we need to evaluate most, if not all, activities, even the companies or sectors that we think do not fit into sustainability, and be practical about it. That is the practical justification for ESG factors. We also need impact, as we need to assess the positive and negative contributions of all those activities, and that is why ESG criteria and impact can become complementary. ESG is a set metric that aims to fit existing assets, while impact investing is a more holistic strategy. Needless to say, the impact is mostly about that impact, be it social and/or environmental, and does not always prioritize financial gain as part of its aims.

BEST-IN-CLASS

Another interesting way to integrate ESG factors is best-in-class. As one can imagine, best-in-class can be defined as the champion or superior element when assessed or filtered by precise characteristics within a certain category. This does not mean, however, that it's the best overall, but it is the best for that criterion or filter. One can choose best in the sector, best in the universe or best efforts, or best progress. What this means is that sometimes we not only choose within our complete universe, but, actually, we build up some criteria to better assess the champions of specific criteria or with specific characteristics. Typical examples of best-in-class assessment can include:

1 Best in sector
2 Best in industry
3 Best in market
4 Best effort or best progress

As we can observe, the assessment of best-in-class can also be performed by effort or progress. In the case of certain specific assets, mostly alternative assets such as securities and real estate, this sort of assessment allows for evaluation of the progress of their efforts. This means that the assessment can be performed within a certain asset class or for the same issuer or asset over multiple periods of time, a practice commonly known as horizontal analysis in accounting.

EXCLUSIONS AND SCREENING

SF has come a long way from the days when it mostly meant not buying the shares of companies in controversial industries. The typical examples were industries dealing with products such as tobacco, firearms, alcohol, or gambling, but the list could go longer sometimes. Exclusions or negative screening were and perhaps still are paramount to screening mainly because they were easy to implement. If we go back and remember how it was some decades ago, even without the use of computers, negative screening was still possible. An investor would just not invest in something that would not align with their values or beliefs.

Research in the field of negative screening was sometimes linked to the concept of sin stocks. In there, we can find arguments such *as "sin stocks are less held by certain institutions, such as pension plans (but not by mutual funds which are natural arbitrageurs), and less followed by analysts than other stocks"* (Hong & Kacperczyk, 2009). And perhaps that quote clearly summarizes the essential problem with exclusions. As some investments are avoided by a number of investors, on one side, we observe censorship and perhaps less efficient reactions from the market are promoted, but, at the same time, arbitrage opportunities can arise for the rest of the investors that do not abide by those rules.

NORMS-BASED SCREENING

Screening, however, can also be positive. It is not as simple as avoiding what is not desired, and it does require a proactive assessment of alternatives to make an investment decision. Norm-based screening can be a great example of this. Investors who support this approach regularly consider a broad range of corporate behavior under the umbrella of certain moral criteria or religious values, also known as faith-based investment. Faith-based investors want returns, as any other investor. They just select investments that align with their religious beliefs and values. This selection can be exclusionary or priority, depending on their mandate. It is also customary that they opt out of investments that might be considered immoral, such as those described in negative screening, but their choice of blacklists can be different from others depending on their own value set.

ACTIVE ENGAGEMENT

Active engagement is one very interesting approach to SF. It is perhaps the most complicated of them all because it requires engagement. What this means is basically that an investor should first invest to be able to engage in the decision-making of that company. This is a very productive approach. It does cost a lot of money, and it does take a lot of effort. Engaging in this approach can mean that an investor would even invest in companies that they do not relate to with the intention of bettering them. Engaging with companies on the decisions that matter the most can increase their value by making them more competitive or even profitable. It promotes shareholder engagement. More on active engagement can be found on the website for Robeco.[5]

Although it is sometimes believed that the power of the market is marginal, as an investor would represent only the value of their investment, recent events, i.e., Gamestop and Exxon, can prove how organized action can yield higher presentation either collectively or with the support of big asset managers representing the best interest of their clients with the power of the portfolios they represent.

IN A NUTSHELL

There is huge potential in SF integration in investments, and ESG integration and impact are just typical examples of it. This is still an evolving field, and as regulation is still evolving with regard to how to define and implement SF in investments, it is problematic to isolate evidence from performance for different SF approaches, as it can lead to mixed results sometimes. In any case, interest from investors continues to grow, and there is evidence that some of those approaches, such as ESG integration, can yield positive results for financial assets (Friede, Busch, & Bassen, 2015). Incorporating a more solid analysis of SF in the investment process can be challenging at this stage, but it is worth the effort in the end as the results align with seeking the best interests of investors and stakeholders.

And as can be seen, the ESG factors incorporate additional elements of analysis. They are not better or worse, but different, and it is important to understand them in order to take advantage of the opportunities they offer. Today there are billions of dollars in investments earmarked for the strategies described above and a few others we didn't mention, and to take advantage of those opportunities, it's important to know and understand them. However, all investment strategies, like any other, require intense analysis work that includes quantitative and qualitative elements in order to promote the best decision-making for the investor, but for the company, it is also important to understand them since they generate an area of opportunity highly relevant when seeking to finance its growth and new projects.

DISCUSSION QUESTIONS

1　What is the spectrum of sustainable finance, and where does it fall between traditional finance and philanthropy?
2　Why is it challenging to classify ESG factors?
3　What is impact investing, and what distinguishes it from philanthropy?
4　What is the intentionality of impact investing, and why is it important?
5　What are the four key elements of impact investing according to the GIIN?
6　How does thematic investing differ from traditional investment strategies?
7　What is the goal of thematic investing?
8　What is negative screening?
9　What are some of the challenges in classifying ESG factors, and how does this impact the development of sustainable finance?
10　Can impact investing be considered a form of philanthropy, and how does it differ from traditional finance?

NOTES

1　For further reference, go to the following link: https://www.sustainablefinance.ch/upload/cms/user/201712_Handbook_on_Sustainable_Investments_CFA.pdf
2　The CFA Institute is a global, not-for-profit professional organization that provides investment professionals with finance education. The institute aims to promote standards in ethics, education, and professional excellence in the global investment services industry. See: https://www.cfainstitute.org/
3　At the time this book was written, the AUM portfolio of Blackrock represented over US$10.01 trillion, according to Google.
4　For further detail on Principles of Responsible Investment see Chapter 9.
5　For further reference, see https://www.robeco.com/us/strategies/solutions/voting-engagement.html

WORKS CITED

Blackrock. (2023). *Thematic investing with BlackRock and iShares*. Retrieved January 2023, from https://www.blackrock.com/lu/individual/themes/thematic-investing/why-invest-thematically

CFA Institute. (2023). *ESG Investing and Analysis*. Retrieved January 2023, from https://www.cfainstitute.org/en/research/esg-investing

Charles Schwab. (2023). *What is thematic investing?* Retrieved January 2023, from https://www.schwab.com/learn/story/what-is-thematic-investing

Friede, G., Busch, T., & Bassen, A. (2015). ESG and financial performance: aggregated evidence from more than 2000 empirical studies. *Journal of Sustainable Finance & Investment, 5*(4), 210–233.

Global Impact Investment Network. (n.d.). *What you need to know about impact investing*. Retrieved January 2022, from https://thegiin.org/impact-investing/need-to-know/

Global Impact Investing Network. (2019, April 3). *Core characteristics of impact investing*. Retrieved January 2022, from https://thegiin.org/assets/Core%20Characteristics_webfile.pdf

Hockerts, K., Hehenberger, L., Schaltegger, S., & Farber, V. (2022). Defining and conceptualizing impact investing: Attractive nuisance or catalyst? *Journal of Business Ethics, 179*(4), 937–950.

Hong, H., & Kacperczyk, M. (2009). The price of sin: The effects of social norms on markets. *Journal of Finance Economics, 93*(1), 15–36.

Howard-Grenville, J. (2021, January 22). ESG impact is hard to measure—but it's not impossible. *Harvard Business Review*.

K. K. (2018, April 17). *The Economist explains*. Retrieved January 16, 2022, from What is sustainable finance? https://www.economist.com/the-economist-explains/2018/04/17/what-is-sustainable-finance?utm_medium=cpc.adword.pd&utm_source=google&ppccampaignID=19495686130&ppcadID=&utm_campaign=a.22brand_pmax&utm_content=conversion.direct-response.anonymous&gclid=Cj0KCQ

Kumar, S., Sharma, D., Rao, S., Lim, W., & Mangla, S. (2022). Past, present, and future of sustainable finance: insights from big data analytics through machine learning of scholarly research. *Annals of Operations Research*. https://doi.org/10.1007/s10479-021-04410-8

Kumar Deshpande, R. (2021). Recent trends in sustainable finance. *Elementary Education Online, 20*(1), 5845–5863.

Nicholls, A. (n.d.). *Sustainable finance: A primer and recent developments*. Asian Development Bank (ADB). Retrieved January 16, 2022, from https://www.adb.org/sites/default/files/institutional-document/691951/ado2021bp-sustainable-finance.pdf

PRI. (n.d.). *ESG integration techniques*. Retrieved January 2023, from https://www.unpri.org/listed-equity/esg-integration-techniques-for-equity-investing/11.article

Rodin, J., & Brandenburg, M. (2014). *The power of impact investing: Putting markets to work for profit and global good*. Philadelphia, PA: Wharton School Press.

State Street Global Advisors. (2022, November). *State Street Global Advisors' Approach to ESG screening*. Retrieved from https://www.ssga.com/library-content/pdfs/insights/esg-screening-piece.pdf

Valliammal, M., & Manivannan, S. (2022). Big data analytics insights of past research on sustainable finance. *Journal For Basic Sciences, 22*(12), 537–548.

World Economic Forum. (n.d.). *Top 10 risks global risks report 2023*. Retrieved from https://www3.weforum.org/docs/WEF_Global_Risks_Report_2023.pdf

CHAPTER 5

The basics of reporting

THE ALPHABET SOUP OF ESG

Reporting is essential for sustainable finance (SF). In fact, reporting is one of those topics that we hear about a lot in the news lately because it is the heart and soul of what we need to figure out to be able to establish fairgrounds and transparency in SF. Reporting is essential for SF because we need the information to be able to run an analysis. The problem is that at first glance, we see and now for that soup into all the acronyms, criteria, definitions, etc., around reporting. For reporting, we need to learn a new language. We have frameworks and standards, while other information suppliers have categories of their own. On top of that, a lot of players in the reporting arena are consolidating, and this is very much expected, as reporting needs to come to a general agreement and understanding of what should be reported, as we find evidence in research that declares that some of those standards are sometimes not consistent with each other (Berg, Koelbel, & Rigobon, 2022).

If there are many frameworks and standards, what do they have in common? In general, most of them support the concept of double materiality (Adams et al., 2021), meaning that they agree on the relevance of certain financial and sustainability metrics that are paramount to the report. Perhaps, most, if not all, standards and frameworks also build on the expectation that disclosures will become mandatory sooner rather than later. And as mentioned above, there is a movement toward the consolidation of different standards and frameworks.

Double materiality considers that the company should report financial, social, and environmental elements jointly. Double materiality is an extension of the accounting concept of materiality for financial information (Täger, 2021), as Figure 5.1 shows double materiality as two opposing prongs. Others propose the concept of double materiality to be understood as a two-way street between the company and its context (social and environmental), as can be observed in Figure 5.2.

VALUE CHAIN OF GHG EMISSIONS

The value chain of GHG (greenhouse gas) emissions refers to the total amount of GHG emissions produced throughout the entire value chain of a product or service, from the extraction of raw materials to production, distribution, use, and disposal.

DOI: 10.4324/9781003274735-5

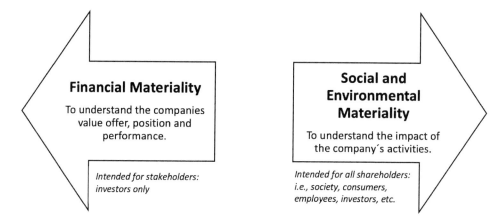

FIGURE 5.1 Double materiality.

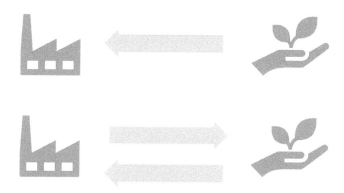

FIGURE 5.2 Materiality versus double materiality.

The value chain of GHG emissions includes all direct and indirect emissions, including carbon dioxide (CO_2), methane (CH_4), nitrous oxide (N_2O), and fluorinated gases (HFCs, PFCs, and SF6) that are released during the various stages of the value chain.

Understanding the value chain of GHG emissions is essential for organizations to identify the major sources of emissions and develop strategies to reduce their carbon footprint. By measuring and reducing the value chain of GHG emissions, companies can minimize their environmental impact and demonstrate their commitment to sustainability.

Please see Scopes for Emissions in Chapter 11.

WHAT TO REPORT?

To use metrics effectively, we need to approach the task systematically. This involves defining the purpose of the reporting and setting priorities, tracking progress, and defining specific goals within those targets. We also need to strategize what we need to do and what behaviors we can expect. Once we start reporting, we can assess ourselves against peer companies and

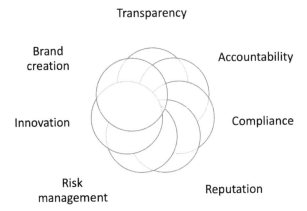

FIGURE 5.3 Reasons for reporting.

find out how we're doing with other companies in the same industry. There are different benchmarks to take into consideration. It is important to understand our audience and what they are looking for in the report. Standardization is important for making the information manageable, relevant, timely, and clear. When it comes to nonstandard metrics, it is also important to include them as part of the report as long as they are collected properly and indexed. While standardized metrics are easier to follow, nonstandard metrics can also help us track a goal or progress.

WHY TO REPORT?

Reporting sustainability is important for transparency and accountability, compliance with legal and voluntary frameworks, enhancing reputation and brand, managing ESG (environmental, social, and governance) risks, identifying areas of innovation and opportunity, and attracting investment and support for sustainability initiatives. Some reasons for reporting can be seen in Figure 5.3.

HOW TO REPORT?

The reporting agencies allow the issuer to format their report however they want but require strict labeling of information to make it easy to find the relevant information. However, companies with multiple subsidiaries have multiple reporting requirements, and it can be challenging to consolidate them. Some companies consolidate all the information and report only one, while others report independently or mix the information. The complexity of reporting depends on the company's size and structure. Small companies with structures like Siemens can find it challenging to create reports for multiple subsidiaries, but for Siemens, it is manageable because of its scale. Regulations on reporting may vary, depending on what kind of regulation is designed. The following are the steps involved in developing metrics for a business:

Identify the purpose of the metrics: The first step is to determine why you need the metrics and what you hope to achieve by measuring them. This could be anything from tracking progress toward a goal to identifying areas for improvement.

Identify the audience: The next step is to identify who will be using the metrics and what information they need. This could include internal stakeholders such as managers and employees, as well as external stakeholders such as investors, customers, and regulators.

Identify the stakeholders: Stakeholders are individuals or groups who have an interest or stake in the business and can influence or be influenced by its actions. They can be internal or external to the organization. Internal stakeholders include employees, managers, shareholders, and other members of the organization. External stakeholders include customers, suppliers, regulators, and the community at large.

Once you have identified the purpose of the metrics, the audience, and the stakeholders, you can begin to develop specific metrics that are tailored to meet the needs of each group. This may involve collecting data, defining metrics, setting targets, and reporting results. It is important to regularly review and update the metrics to ensure that they continue to provide relevant and useful information for decision-making.

METRICS

Identify and select metrics

When selecting metrics, it is important to consider manageability, relevance, timeliness, and clarity. By doing so, it can be ensured that the metrics selected provide meaningful insights and enable effective decision-making. Key characteristics of metrics can be observed in Figure 5.4.

Manageable: The selected metrics should be manageable, meaning that they can be easily tracked and measured within the available resources and time frame. It is recommended to select metrics that can be collected easily and inexpensively.

Relevant: The metrics chosen should be relevant to the goals and objectives of the project or organization. They should reflect the key performance indicators (KPIs) that are important for success.

Timely: The metrics should be timely, meaning that they can be measured and reported on a regular basis, such as weekly or monthly. This allows for timely feedback and course correction when needed.

Clear: The metrics should be clear and easily understood by all stakeholders. They should be presented in a way that is easy to interpret and analyze.

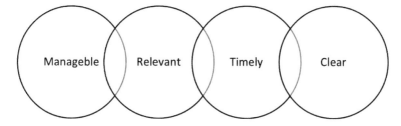

FIGURE 5.4 Key characteristics of metrics.

TABLE 5.1 Major sustainability reporting standards and frameworks

Standard/Framework		Focus	Founded	Link
GRI	Global Reporting Initiative (Global Reporting Initiative, 2023)	Environmental, social	1997	https://www.globalreporting.org/
CDP	CDP Worldwide (CDP, 2023)	Carbon, water, forests	2000	https://www.cdp.net/en/
PRI	Principles for Responsible Investment (UNEP Finance, 2023)	Financial, environmental, social	2005	https://www.unpri.org/
CDSB	Climate Disclosure Standards Board* (IFRS Foundation, 2023a)	Climate change and natural capital	2007	https://www.ifrs.org/sustainability/climate-disclosure-standards-board/
IR	Integrated Reporting* (IFRS Foundation, 2023b)	Financial, environmental, and social	2010	https://www.integratedreporting.org/
SASB	Sustainability Accounting Standards Board* (IFRS Foundation, 2023c)	Sustainability accounting, Environmental, social, and corporate governance	2011	https://www.sasb.org/
TCFD	Task Force on Climate-Related Financial Disclosures (Task Force on Climate-related Financial Disclosures, 2023)	Climate change	2015	https://www.fsb-tcfd.org/

* Part of IFRS Foundation.

DIFFERENT SUSTAINABILITY REPORTING STANDARDS

As sustainability reporting is not yet mandatory in many geographies, there are many alternatives for sustainability reporting, between frameworks and standards. Some of the major ones are shown in Table 5.1, but the most relevant ones are typically regarded as GRI, The Task Force on Climate-related Financial Disclosures (TCFD), The Sustainability Accounting Standards Board SASB, and CDP (originally established as Carbon Disclosure Project), in no particular order.

TCFD, GRI, CDP, and SASB

Some of these standards and frameworks display their own unique understanding, and this should not come as a surprise. There are different manners to approach the same objective, and that shows from these standards and frameworks. For example, GRI is known to be a very popular standard that depicts high complexity and good investor relevance, but they are not always as comprehensive as others. TCFD is a framework that is also technically complex, but not so popular from the investor side but very well accepted by financial institutions and regulators as they align well with financial disclosures. CDP is a special case as a framework that sets the standard for disclosures on carbon, water, and forests in a simple way that might be somehow relevant for investors and gain good popular acceptance (Maywald, 2020).

Standards set the basic level of minimum required information to be reported. That minimum has to be defined so that it is acceptable and relevant. And disclosed information will have to be as detailed as possible.

Frameworks offer context for information. Frameworks are usually suppletory to standards. A framework is more flexible that a standard as they are more similar to a set of principles or guidance.

FIGURE 5.5 Difference between standards and frameworks.

But what is the difference between standards and frameworks, and why would we need both? As we can see in Figure 5.5, there are some differences, but there might be no perfect answer, as, basically, organizations that provide their own frameworks, standards, or guiding principles choose how to label them. And sometimes, they even have issues with all of the above, so the line can get blurry in some cases.

Frameworks and standards should have a clear objective and be independent and even promote third-party verification for their due process to generate a stronger foundation for information to be reported and reliable.

WHAT ABOUT MANDATORY REPORTING?

Europe is perhaps the best case for regulation at this point. They have already advanced into taxonomies and other different regulations to describe what SF should be and what to disclose about it.

In the United States, the Securities and Exchange Commission (SEC) is the one responsible for proposing regulation, and this includes the generalities of disclosures and reporting rules on climate change for the United States. This is a rather ambitious goal in a global world where investors themselves already expect this kind of response from every market they participate in and where the United States was not the trailblazer. The main argument for this delay is the potential impact on operations or financial conditions for American companies, while multinationals already face these in other markets.

Regulators are not unaware of climate risks, and many acknowledge the fact that those risks can represent financial risks for companies, and that is the big argument here. We just need to understand how to align them to regulation. Investors need reliable information to make informed investment decisions, they urge it, and they even get it in any case. And all parties benefit from clear rules. The demand for consistent and comparable information that can affect financial performance exists, and the SEC plays a critical role in this.

As regulation continues to advance and is soon to become mandatory in the United States as well, it is certain financial statement metrics related to the climate, such as reports of GHG emissions, among other things, will soon be more standard, and that is a significant gain for the financial market. It is a good step in the right direction, but it still leaves some issues related to their real impact, which is clearly more difficult to measure, report, and compare, pending. But that will have to be a fight for another day.

For Europe, the main concern seems to be greenwashing, while the United States, and particularly the SEC, seems to be more interested in risk, the environmental risk, to be more precise. And those topics are today in the central part of the discussion, and it is something that is also widely recognized. For entities that already carry out stress tests and other risk assessments, this is not even an imposition, as they already do it. We will just have to wait and see how it gets implemented.

THE EU AND SF

The European Community has been taking significant steps toward promoting SF by introducing regulatory frameworks aimed at steering investments toward environmentally sustainable projects. The European Commission's Action Plan on Financing Sustainable Growth, published in March 2018, outlined a range of initiatives aimed at mobilizing private capital toward sustainable investments and establishing a regulatory framework that promotes SF.

One of the key initiatives introduced under the Action Plan is the creation of a classification system for sustainable economic activities, known as the EU Taxonomy. The EU Taxonomy is a comprehensive system that sets out criteria for economic activities that can be considered sustainable. The system classifies economic activities according to their contribution to six environmental objectives: climate change mitigation, climate change adaptation, sustainable use and protection of water and marine resources, transition to a circular economy, pollution prevention and control, and protection and restoration of biodiversity and ecosystems.

Another key regulatory framework introduced by the European Community to promote SF is the Sustainable Finance Disclosure Regulation (SFDR). The SFDR requires financial market participants and financial advisors to disclose the extent to which sustainability risks are integrated into their investment decision-making process. The regulation also requires disclosure of the impact of sustainability factors on investment decisions and the transparency of the products offered to investors.

The European Community has also introduced the Regulation on Low Carbon Benchmarks, which aims to encourage the development and use of low-carbon benchmarks by investors. This regulation sets out the requirements for low-carbon benchmarks and promotes the use of these benchmarks as a way to measure the performance of investment funds and financial products.

In addition to these regulatory frameworks, the European Community has also established the Platform on SF, which brings together representatives from the financial industry, civil society, and academia to advise the European Commission on SF issues.

THE SEC AND SF

The SEC in the United States has been taking steps toward promoting SF by introducing regulatory frameworks aimed at guiding investments toward environmentally sustainable projects. The SEC has recognized that SF can play an important role in addressing climate change and promoting ESG factors.

In March 2021, the SEC announced the creation of a Climate and ESG Task Force to identify and analyze ESG-related misconduct in the securities industry. The task force is part of the SEC's broader effort to assess how companies are responding to the growing demand for disclosure of ESG risks and opportunities.

One of the key initiatives introduced by the SEC to promote SF is the adoption of ESG disclosure requirements. In 2020, the SEC proposed amendments to the regulation, which requires companies to disclose material information in their SEC filings. The proposed amendments would require companies to disclose information about their ESG risks and opportunities, including climate change risk, in their public filings.

The SEC has also issued interpretive guidance to assist public companies in complying with the existing disclosure requirements related to climate change. In 2010, the SEC issued interpretive guidance on climate change disclosure, which clarified that companies should disclose material climate change risks and opportunities in their public filings.

In addition to disclosure requirements, the SEC has also introduced a regulatory framework to guide investment advisors in their consideration of ESG factors. The SEC's Division of Investment Management issued a guidance update in 2020, which clarifies how investment advisors should integrate ESG factors into their investment decisions. The guidance update emphasizes the importance of considering material ESG factors and provides a framework for investment advisors to evaluate ESG factors in the context of their clients' investment objectives.

IN A NUTSHELL

There are different alternatives to reporting. Currently, the best-known standards and frameworks are usually understood well by experts according to what they offer but are a bit trickier to steer for the public. As reporting becomes mandatory, some issues will be resolved. Sustainability today is as relevant as finance for corporations, and data will need to be collected, analyzed, and eventually audited. Sustainability will become part of companies' annual reporting process, and while that gets regulated, we will have to rely on frameworks, principles, standards, and other guidance to do our part.

DISCUSSION QUESTIONS

1 What is the importance of reporting and disclosure?
2 Why do we need to learn a new language for reporting in sustainable finance?
3 What is double materiality?
4 What are the key characteristics of relevant metrics for reporting?
5 What are the major sustainability reporting standards and frameworks?
6 What are the differences between the major sustainability reporting standards and frameworks?
7 What are the main differences in regulations related to reporting in Europe and the United States?
8 Why is the consolidation of reporting standards and frameworks necessary for SF reporting?

9 How do sustainability reporting standards and frameworks help promote transparency and fairgrounds in sustainable finance?

10 What challenges do companies face when trying to implement sustainability reporting and comply with reporting standards and frameworks?

WORKS CITED

Adams, C. A., Alhamood, A., He, X., Tian, J., Wang, L., & Wang, Y. (2021). *The double-materiality concept: Application and issues.* GRI.

Berg, F., Koelbel, J. F., & Rigobon, R. (2022). Aggregate confusion: The divergence of ESG ratings. *Review of Finance, 26*(6), 1315–1344.

CDP. (2023). *CDP.* Retrieved from https://www.cdp.net/en/

Global Reporting Initiative. (2023). *Global Reporting Initiative.* Retrieved from https://www.globalreporting.org/

IFRS Foundation. (2023a). *Climate Disclosure Standards Board.* Retrieved from https://www.ifrs.org/sustainability/climate-disclosure-standards-board/

IFRS Foundation. (2023b). *Integrated reporting.* Retrieved from https://www.integratedreporting.org/

IFRS Foundation. (2023c). *SASB standards.* Retrieved from https://www.sasb.org/

Maywald, D. (2020, April 7). *The reporting landscape is rapidly changing for sustainable investment and ESG disclosures.* Retrieved from https://www.linkedin.com/pulse/reporting-landscape-rapidly-changing-sustainable-esg-david/

Täger, M. (2021, April 20). *'Double materiality': What is it and why does it matter?* Retrieved January 2022, from https://www.lse.ac.uk/granthaminstitute/news/double-materiality-what-is-it-and-why-does-it-matter/

Task Force on Climate-related Financial Disclosures. (2023). *Task Force on Climate-related Financial Disclosures.* Retrieved from https://www.fsb-tcfd.org/

UNEP Finance. (2023). *Principles of Responsible Investment.*

CHAPTER 6

Equity ownership

TYPES OF EQUITY INVESTMENT

There are different kinds of equities. In general terms, private and public equity (Moon, 2006). Those two categories can be observed in Figure 6.1. And it is important to highlight here that private companies do not publicly disclose their information but still need to incorporate sustainability. For private companies, investors have closer contact with the company, and they have much more influence on them (Weir, Jones, & Wright, 2015). But private companies are more hermetic when disclosing their information, and only those that are in the know are the ones that are going to get access to information. Most of the information that the company would disclose might be just basic fundamental financial information, but it should be enough to keep investors comfortable about the performance of their investment. The kind of information that will allow you to understand whether your investment makes sense.

Proxy voting

How do we communicate with the markets? How do we engage as investors in the markets? For most investors, it will be through proxy voting.

> Proxy vote refers to a ballot cast by a single person or firm on behalf of a corporation's shareholder who may not be able to attend a shareholder meeting, or who may not choose to vote on a particular issue. Shareholders receive a proxy ballot in the mail, and an information booklet called a proxy statement, which describes the issues to be voted on during the meeting. Shareholders vote on a variety of issues including the election of board members, merger or acquisition approvals, or approving a stock compensation plan.
>
> (Kenton, n.d.)

Although it might not be the hottest approach to engage as investors in our investments, it's an efficient way to approach it. It is practical. Many investors never get to see themselves casting votes on boards of companies they hold stock in (Maug & Rydqvist, 2001). And that is the result of many things, i.e., because you have thousands of investors, and it is not practical just

DOI: 10.4324/9781003274735-6

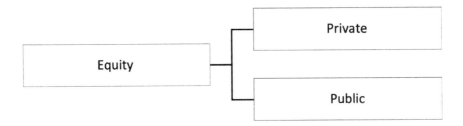

FIGURE 6.1 Types of equity.

to gather all of them together at the same place or even at the same time. It is also complicated because those investors are in different places with different time zones even. But also, because a lot of annual meetings also take place at the same time of the year. And even if you made it through all those complications and you were able to make it to every single annual meeting you must attend, you would also have to be knowledgeable of the issues at hand, which would also require an extra outlay of time to be committed to every single vote to be cast. Now imagine investors typically diversify and might be invested in more than a handful of companies. Then multiply the number of companies in their portfolios by all that time commitment and logistics juggling for each company. Eventually, it ends up being a full-time job. And some of those investors might not be able to actively cast their votes directly for every single company they invest in. In the end, much voting will happen through proxy voting as it becomes significantly more practical.

Proxy voting allows you to cast your vote in absence, and you do it according to specific criteria. If your stake in a company is relatively small, chances are your asset manager is making those decisions for the client to remove the hassle from you. But as you start to have considerable holdings in a particular company, you get the opportunity to have a bigger say in that vote. You perhaps are interested in selecting the direction your vote will be cast in. Why is this important? Just because that is how we promote sustainability in finance. When you get a questionnaire regarding your interest in different topics voted in an annual assembly, and you declare your response to other issues voted for in the community, you influence the direction you would prefer for your vote to be cast in. You become an engaged owner of your assets. And that is a good thing. Those votes will count, and in the aggregate, more stockholders with similar interests will lever the balance toward a better direction.

Some companies offer their services for proxy voting. These proxy voting companies can also give investors advice on what's in their best interest to vote according to different criteria that you pre-establish or just to nudge you into different directions according to certain standards, general criteria, or their own expertise. But ultimately, investors keep the power to choose what kind of direction they go in on their voting.

So what can we expect in the future? Is it going to continue to be like this? I would think so. With the advance of technology, more and more will see these opportunities precisely. What would be the point of voting on individual issues if you could just define the criteria in general and trust that a third party will take care of the rest. Your vote would be aligned with what you already have specified anyway.

EQUITY VALUATION

Valuation in equity deploys different methodologies from traditional finance, i.e., discounted cash flows, absolute valuation, etc. The choice of methodology usually depends on the kind of information that is available. Some methodologies are more precise, while others are just more practical to use. However, sometimes those methodologies might not be the most precise as they miss to consider intangibles, and ESG (environmental, social and governance) factors and sustainability are typical examples of it. Studies show that intangibles are a very significant element of valuation for companies (Zéghal & Maaloul, 2011), at least for public companies for which we have the most data available, but certainly also for private companies that cannot be excluded from that trend. That's why we use relative valuation methods, i.e., multiples. This sort of methodology incorporates not only the financial fundamentals of the company but also the apparent value of the company from market quotes or other benchmarks. By this approach, we incorporate not only internal data from the financial reports of the company but also external data about their stock price on the market. Some examples of these include earnings per share, price ratios, etc. Those are the typical ones, but also multiples that give you a reference point to understand how many times the value of a company should represent its potential are relevant. Multiples vary by geography and industry (Zéghal & Maaloul, 2011). For calculating them, we have to assess how to use the data reported according to standards for a fair valuation. Because once you get the multiples, you do not use it for comparisons right away, not even two that you would find to be identical at first glance, as every company has its own complexities. You would have to do a little more work on how you prepare your analysis, and you also must be able to fine-tune those calculations to get something useful.

Let us think of very basic examples. Comparing the two most famous beverage companies, two of the most popular streaming services, or even a pair of airlines. No matter how similar each pair of companies looks, there are always going to be complexities that make them different. For example, each company in a set might be in the same line of business, but their business strategy might differ, or they may be operating in different geographies or even be reporting according to different accounting standards. Each company ends up being unique, and its uniqueness needs to be addressed in its assessment.

ESG and impact

Nowadays, we find companies that report under ESG criteria everywhere. Every big enough respectable company complies with the ESG criteria because it's expected from them. This is because there are going to be opportunities resulting from it, but also because it is basically the new standard. So we start to see how ESG criteria become part of the valuation for different assets. And we see how some markets start to show reasonable prices, while others heat up and become overpriced. A typical example of fairly priced assets according to this criterion can be found in some countries in Europe, while China sometimes exhibits tricky valuations with high ESG risk levels and high valuations. Usually, the United States offers an interesting mix of value and opportunity, but that is just a general case, and a case-by-case situation needs to be assessed.

If you were to convert that into something more simple to understand in financial terms, that is the kind of analysis you do with interest. It's a matter of what the claim is as a percentage. How much interest you get paid and how much an investment you have to make to get the kind of payment you get once you convert it to a percentage is straightforward to read and clear to understand. Same thing as the price-earnings ratio. How much are those earnings? Are they representing the price of the asset that you're investing in? What do we see here? There is a whole universe out there. It doesn't mean that opportunities exist everywhere. It means that many options exist. It might be something like this on global markets and aggregate the rebound on average. What happened for these companies was faster for those regarded as highly unsustainable, or it can also be that you can find exciting opportunities in different geographies. For example, it's essential to understand how. This balance exists, yes, because, in reality, we're going to see that there are many options and lots of opportunities that we can get. What's the exciting part of right now? We can now choose where to go and what kind of investments to make according to the different criteria. We want to follow all the values that we can assign or align to our assets. Shareholders matter, they take most of the risk, and that is why we will talk about equity. Long-term value also requires investors who commit to companies and benefits.

For more on how to incorporate sustainability into equity, please refer to Chapter 4.

Bridging sustainability and equity. How accurate or comparable are ratings?

The short answer is not very much (Berg, Koelbel, & Rigobon, 2022). ESG ratings are used to evaluate the sustainability and responsible business practices of companies and are becoming increasingly important for investors and stakeholders in decision-making processes. However, the accuracy and comparability of ESG ratings can vary widely, depending on several factors, i.e., first, there is a lack of standardization in ESG data collection and reporting, which can result in inconsistent ratings across different providers. This is because ESG data is often self-reported by companies, which can lead to variations in the quality and reliability of the data. Furthermore, different ESG rating providers may have different methodologies and weightings of ESG factors, which can result in varying ratings for the same company.

Second, ESG ratings are often based on publicly available information, which may not capture the full picture of a company's ESG performance. For example, a company may have strong ESG practices that are not reflected in its public disclosures or may be working on improving its ESG performance but may not have achieved measurable results yet.

Third, ESG rating providers may face conflicts of interest, as they may receive payment from the companies they rate or may have commercial relationships with them. This can create potential biases in the ratings and reduce their objectivity.

While ESG ratings can be useful tools for evaluating the sustainability and responsible business practices of companies, it is important to recognize their limitations and potential biases. It is also important to use multiple sources of information and to take a critical approach when evaluating ESG ratings to ensure that they are accurate and comparable.

WHY DOES SUSTAINABILITY MATTER FOR EQUITY?

Sustainability matters for equity because it creates value for companies, which in turn can lead to better financial performance and investment returns. By integrating ESG factors into their business models and operations, companies can improve their competitive position, reduce risks, and increase efficiency, ultimately leading to higher profitability and shareholder value.

Additionally, sustainable investing is becoming increasingly popular among investors who want to align their financial goals with their personal values. Investors are looking for companies that demonstrate a commitment to sustainability and responsible business practices and are willing to invest in those companies that meet their criteria. This can lead to increased demand for shares of companies that prioritize sustainability, driving up their stock prices and creating positive returns for investors.

Sustainability also has a wider impact on society and the environment. By investing in sustainable companies, investors can support efforts to reduce carbon emissions, conserve natural resources, promote social justice and equity, and address other important societal and environmental issues.

Long-term value

Companies that align their business strategies with ESG factors can create additional value and competitive advantages. Integrating sustainability into a company's DNA can also lead to greater efficiency, lower costs, and access to more financing options. However, the success of implementing ESG strategies is dependent on the type of company and the intentionality behind the efforts. While some companies are leaders in sustainability, others may unintentionally achieve good results. It is also important for companies to disclose their efforts to achieve ESG goals. Overall, ESG factors can positively impact a company's performance and benefit both the company and its stakeholders.

SHAREHOLDERS AND STAKEHOLDERS

Shareholders and stakeholders are two groups of individuals or entities that have an interest in a company or organization, but they differ in their relationship and level of involvement with the company (Adams, Licht, & Sagiv, 2011).

Shareholders are individuals or entities that own a share or shares in a company. They are typically investors who provide capital to the company in exchange for ownership and have a financial interest in the success of the company. Shareholders are entitled to receive a portion of the profits in the form of dividends and may have voting rights on certain company decisions, such as electing the board of directors.

Stakeholders, on the other hand, are individuals or entities that are affected by or have an interest in the activities of the company, but they do not necessarily have a financial interest in the company. Stakeholders can include employees, customers, suppliers, local communities, and the environment. They are impacted by the actions of the company and may have expectations or demands for the company to act in a socially responsible and ethical manner.

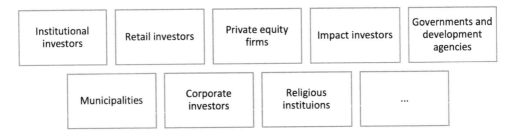

FIGURE 6.2 Typical examples of potential investors in SF.

The main difference between shareholders and stakeholders is that shareholders have a direct financial interest in the company, while stakeholders have an indirect interest and are affected by the company's actions in various ways. Shareholders primarily focus on the financial success of the company, while stakeholders may have broader concerns, such as social and environmental impact.

Who is investing in sustainable finance (SF)?

Pretty much everybody, as there is a growing interest in SF from various types of investors, including those mentioned in Figure 6.2.

And the list can go on. SF has become a mainstream investment strategy, and investors across various sectors and geographies are increasingly recognizing the importance of investing in a more sustainable future.

Stakeholder capitalism

Stakeholder capitalism (Freeman, Martin, & Parmar, 2007) is an economic system in which companies prioritize the interests of all stakeholders, including employees, customers, suppliers, communities, and the environment, in addition to shareholders. This approach emphasizes the idea that businesses have a responsibility to create value not just for their shareholders but also for society as a whole. Stakeholder capitalism differs from the traditional model of shareholder capitalism, which places the interests of shareholders above that of all other stakeholders. In shareholder capitalism, the primary goal of a corporation is to maximize shareholder value and profits, often at the expense of other stakeholders.

Stakeholder capitalism has gained popularity in recent years as a response to growing concerns about income inequality, climate change, and the role of corporations in society. Advocates argue that companies that prioritize the interests of all stakeholders are more likely to create sustainable long-term value and contribute to a healthier and more equitable society.

Conscious capitalism

Conscious capitalism (Mackey & Sisodia, 2014) is a business philosophy that emphasizes the importance of serving all stakeholders in a company, including employees, customers, suppliers, and the community, as well as shareholders. The concept was first introduced by John Mackey, the co-founder and CEO of Whole Foods Market, and Raj Sisodia, a marketing professor.

Conscious capitalism aims to create a more sustainable and ethical business model that is focused on creating value for all stakeholders rather than just maximizing profits for shareholders. This involves creating a culture of trust, collaboration, and empathy, and treating employees as partners in the business, rather than as resources to be exploited. Some of the key principles of conscious capitalism include purpose, stakeholder orientation, conscious leadership, conscious culture, and conscious management (Mackey & Sisodia, 2014). Conscious capitalism represents a shift away from the traditional business model that prioritizes short-term profits over long-term sustainability and ethical behavior. Instead, it aims to create a more inclusive and sustainable business model that creates value for all stakeholders.

EMERGING ALTERNATIVES AND EVOLUTION OF ESG

ESG is not the only way to go with SF. As described previously, other standpoints also exist, including impact and several others mentioned ahead.

Science-based targets initiative (SBTi)[1]

Science-based targets (SBTs) are greenhouse gas emissions reduction targets that are aligned with the latest climate science necessary to limit global warming to well below 2°C above pre-industrial levels, as set out in the Paris Agreement. The SBTi is a collaboration between CDP (originally established as Carbon Disclosure Project), the United Nations Global Compact (UNGC), World Resources Institute (WRI), and the World Wide Fund (WWF). SBTi provides a framework and guidance to companies for setting and achieving SBTs (Andersen et al., 2021).

SBTi encourages companies to set targets that are consistent with what the latest climate science indicates is necessary to meet the Paris Agreement's goals. Specifically, companies must set targets that aim to limit their emissions so that they do not exceed the level of emissions required to keep global warming below 1.5°C or well below 2°C above pre-industrial levels. SBTi also requires companies to periodically report their progress toward achieving their targets and provide evidence that their targets are based on science and are consistent with a fair share of the global emissions reduction effort. Will this be the perfect solution? It is still too early to know (Giesekam, Norman, Garvey, & Betts-Davies, 2021).

TYPICAL MISCONCEPTIONS REGARDING SF IN EQUITY

SF has gained momentum in recent years, but there are still several misconceptions surrounding this concept. Let's address some of them:

Misconception 1: There is no evidence to support that SFs offer competitive returns.

Many investors are hesitant to invest in SF because they believe it will hurt their bottom line. However, this is a misconception. Research has shown that SF can offer competitive returns and, in some cases, even outperform traditional investments. For example, studies have shown that companies with better ESG performance tend to have higher long-term profitability, lower volatility, and lower cost of capital. Additionally, green bonds, which finance environmentally friendly projects, have been shown to offer similar returns to conventional bonds.

Misconception 2: Environmental regulation regarding the disclosure of information on ESG issues is not there yet.

There has been a growing interest in ESG issues from investors, regulators, and the public. However, there is still a long way to go. Many companies still do not disclose their ESG performance, and there is a lack of standardization in ESG reporting. But this is changing rapidly. In fact, companies that own their narrative regarding ESG disclosure find benefits in early adoption. Even if environmental regulations are often lax or unenforced, which limits the impact of SF, we have seen what the tendency is today in different geographies. And if we account for globalization, effects are experienced globally.

Misconception 3: It is not possible to have both impact and return.

SF aims to generate both financial returns and positive social and environmental impacts. However, there is often a trade-off between the two. For example, investments in renewable energy may generate a lower return compared to investments in fossil fuels. Investors must be realistic about the returns they can expect from SF investments and understand that impact and return are not always perfectly aligned, but they can be achieved.

Misconception 4: Incorporating sustainability in finance benefits investors (fiduciaryresponsibility).

Investment managers have a fiduciary responsibility to act in the best interests of their clients. This includes considering the long-term risks and opportunities associated with ESG issues. Incorporating sustainability in finance can help investors better manage these risks and identify new investment opportunities. Furthermore, investors who prioritize sustainability may attract a growing segment of clients who are concerned about the impact of their investments.

Misconception 5: It is an opportunity that is already a reality worldwide.

SF is still in its early stages, and while it is growing, it is already a reality worldwide. Many investors globally are starting to prioritize sustainability in their investment decisions. However, the lack of standardization in ESG reporting and ratings still limits the comparability of SF investments, but the consolidation of such ratings is also happening fast.

IN A NUTSHELL

SF offers significant potential for generating both financial returns and positive social and environmental impacts. However, there are still several misconceptions surrounding this concept. It is essential to understand the trade-offs between impact and return, the current state of ESG reporting and regulation, and the opportunities and challenges of SF. By doing so, investors can make informed decisions that align with their goals and values.

SF is highly relevant for equity investments. Companies that prioritize sustainability and ESG issues tend to have better long-term financial performance, lower risk, and are more attractive to socially responsible investors. Incorporating sustainability in equity investments can help investors identify opportunities and manage risks, as well as align their investments with their values. Furthermore, SF can help drive positive social and environmental impact, supporting a more equitable and sustainable future. As the world continues to grapple with the challenges of climate change, social inequality, and environmental degradation, SF will become increasingly important in ensuring a more resilient and equitable global economy.

DISCUSSION QUESTIONS

1   What are the different types of equities?
2   Why does sustainability matter for equity?
3   How do private companies disclose information to investors?
4   How does the information disclosed by private companies compare to that disclosed by public companies?
5   How can investors influence the private companies they invest in?
6   What is proxy voting, and why is it important?
7   How do investors engage with the markets through proxy voting?
8   Why is proxy voting necessary?
9   What methodologies are used in equity valuation, and how do they incorporate sustainability and ESG factors?
10 How can equity valuation methods be adapted to better incorporate ESG factors and sustainability considerations?

NOTE

1 For further reference, see https://sciencebasedtargets.org/

WORKS CITED

Adams, R. B., Licht, A. N., & Sagiv, L. (2011). Shareholders and stakeholders: How do directors decide? *Strategic Management Journal, 32*(12), 1331–1355.

Andersen, I., Ishii, N., Brooks, T., Cummis, C., Fonseca, G., Hillers, A., . . . Zimm, C. (2021). Defining 'science-based targets'. *National Science Review, 8*(7), nwaa186.

Berg, F., Koelbel, J. F., & Rigobon, R. (2022). Aggregate confusion: The divergence of ESG ratings. *Review of Finance, 26*(6), 1315–1344.

Freeman, R. E., Martin, K., & Parmar, B. (2007). Stakeholder capitalism. *Journal of Business Ethics, 74*, 303–314.

Giesekam, J., Norman, J., Garvey, A., & Betts-Davies, S. (2021). Science-based targets: On target? *Sustainability, 13*(4), 1657.

Kenton, W. (n.d.). *Investopedia.* Retrieved January 2023, from What is a proxy vote, and how does it work? With examples: https://www.investopedia.com/terms/p/proxy-vote.asp

Mackey, J., & Sisodia, R. (2014). *Conscious capitalism, with a new preface by the authors: Liberating the heroic spirit of business.* Harvard Business Review Press.

Maug, E., & Rydqvist, K. (2001). What is the function of the shareholder meeting? Evidence from the U.S. proxy voting process. Working Paper. Humboldt University and Norwegian School of Management.

Moon, J. J. (2006). Public vs. private equity. *Journal of Applied Corporate Finance, 18*(3), 76–82.

Weir, C., Jones, P., & Wright, M. (2015). Public to private transactions, private equity and financial health in the UK: An empirical analysis of the impact of going private. *Journal of Management & Governance, 19*, 91–112.

Zéghal, D., & Maaloul, A. (2011, December). The accounting treatment of intangibles – A critical review of the literature. *Accounting Forum, 34*(4), 262–274.

CHAPTER 7

Bonds in different colors, shapes, and sizes

THE BASICS OF BONDS

Bonds are financing instruments commonly issued as a form of financing. They can also be known as fixed-income assets when observed from the perspective of investments, as investors acquire them with the purpose of obtaining a return that is assigned at the issuance of the instrument. Bonds are normally backed up by the wealth of the issuer or a specific asset (usually owned by the issuer). Issuers are entities, companies, governments, or other institutions that aim to fund their projects or activities. That is why we need to understand the financial health of the issuer to understand where the risk of a bond stands as the issuer becomes the counterparty to the investor. And so, different bonds can be categorized depending on who issues them, as can be observed in Figure 7.1.

In a way, bonds are not that different from loans, as they have a specific and defined use of proceeds, and money is tended with the intention to be repaid. And so, repayment will be a central element of risk assessment for bonds. Traditional bonds[1] are usually issued to finance their issuers' needs or projects, and that is why the use of proceeds is usually a relevant element of their design. Legal structuring and design of traditional bonds are usually regarded to be solid to allow the design of a reliable investment instrument, and so bonds may be regarded as lower risk than other assets. In this chapter, we will discuss in detail green, social, sustainable, and others (GSS+ bonds).[2]

Bonds operate differently than other traditional assets, i.e., equity. Equity stocks typically pay dividends as a form of retribution to their investors for bearing their investment risk. At the same time, investors can profit from the value they generate from trading on the secondary market, but that value will come at a risk. As equity typically does not offer the same level of surety as bonds, they must pay higher returns to cover for that risk, but at the same time, stocks offer other perks relevant to their investors, i.e., voting rights. And voting rights are one of the critical elements that differentiate stocks from bonds. Bonds do not confer voting rights. And the list can go on. Please see Figure 7.2 for a stylized representation of the main characteristics of stocks and bonds.

In the case of bonds, they are typically regarded to be a bit more secure as an investment than other asset classes. Bonds usually offer a guarantee, being backed by the issuer or by some specific asset owned by the issuer. In addition, as bonds would have any sort of preferential

DOI: 10.4324/9781003274735-7

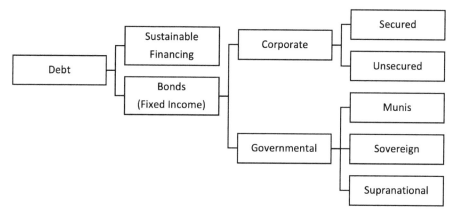

FIGURE 7.1 Types of bonds by issuer.

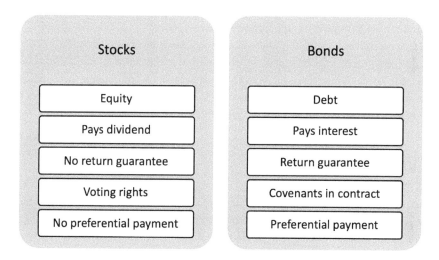

FIGURE 7.2 Selected differences between stocks and bonds.

treatment when the bond matures, creditors usually get preference over investors for repayment. As dividends are the return of stocks, bonds would typically pay interest instead. And a bond investor usually knows the amount of interest to be paid since they acquire the bond. Interest rates for bonds can be either fixed or variable. Fixed interest is when you know exactly how much the coupon or payment for a bond will be, i.e., 2%. At the same time, variable interest is usually represented by a premium that is added to a base rate, i.e., a theoretical prime rate of 4.25% and an added margin of 1%, resulting in 5.25% total rate.

Corporate-issued bonds and government-issued bonds

Who issues bonds? Corporations and governments mainly. Perhaps the most common bonds are issued by corporations, like the ones you know from the stock market, but also some others that do not necessarily trade their stock but choose to go for funding in the fixed-income market. These bonds are traditionally issued to fund the specific needs of that company. A bond could be similar to a contract or an IOU[3] between a lender, creditor, or investor and a borrower or issuer.

There are also bonds issued by government entities that we can call *government-issued bonds*. Among them, we can find different subcategories for government-issued bonds, depending on the branch of government that makes the emission, i.e., Munis, which are bonds emitted by municipalities in the United States. Munis can be somehow risky because they come from diverse issuers that an investor can find on the market. However, as it is with other bonds, the relevant part is to keep in mind who the counterparty is, as counterparties convey a significant part of the risk of a bond. And so, not every municipality or city is the same. We would need to take a closer look.

We also have issuers at the national level, also known as sovereign bonds. A similar case, just at a bigger scale, as no country is the same as the next. An investor may find that some countries can be more trustworthy than others. Not every aspect of the risk of a country might be the same for their peers. And although sometimes you may find countries that are at risk of default, others would be more stable and will do everything they can to keep their credit rating.

Finally, we also have supranational, which considers emissions that account for global programs, i.e., the World Bank, Interamerican Development Bank, and others. Supranational issuers typically sponsor specific regions or programs in different countries, and sometimes they can also be leading issues for bonds in some geographies, i.e., less developed countries.

BOND VALUATION

Bonds are usually valuated by applying the present value formula to their expected interest payments, also known as the bond's cash flow, and the bond's value upon maturity, also known as par or face value. We can see an example in Table 7.1:

For this very simple example, we can see how an investment of US$10,000 is made, marked as a negative to indicate that disbursement was made, and labeled as PV for present value. In the next four boxes, we then find the coupon amount of the bond, in this case, US$500, expected to be the inflows or returns of this instrument, and, finally, payment of the investment value of the bond and the last coupon payment altogether in year 5. It may seem that there is no significant information here. However, we can get from this simple cash flow

TABLE 7.1 An example of bond cash flows

PV	(US$10,000)
1	US$500
2	US$500
3	US$500
4	US$500
5	US$10,500

that the bond had a maturity of five years, a yearly interest rate of 5% (or US$500/US$10,000), and that it was sold at par. As we can see, for this very simplified case, the time value of money is a perfect tool to assess valuation.

Perhaps, the key complexity with bond valuation is that sometimes they have coupons (direct interest rate payments), or sometimes they yield returns at a discount, meaning that they are acquired at a different value than the stated amount that they are issued for, also known as face value. For our previous example in Table 7.1, meaning that we would pay for the bond only (US$9,500) instead of (US$10,000), but still get the US$10,000 in the end and consider this discount as part of the value of the bond. And we do not want to get too technical on this part as it is not the purpose of this chapter, but we should keep in mind that there are different kinds of bonds depending on what returns they yield.

CREDIT RATINGS

Another relevant element to understand with bonds is credit ratings. Bonds are rated according to different factors, mainly risk factors. As we can expect, the counterparty or issuer of the bond is in significant part what is being assessed in an emission; ratings typically look like school grades, letter grades, that is. Going on alphabetical scales, but sometimes just elaborating a bit more on the nomenclature so that rating agencies can give their distinct character to the scale. How does it look? You may find a typical example of a credit rating scale in Figure 7.3.

But there is a bit more complexity in the rating of financial instruments besides their nomenclature. Typically, rating agencies offer their services to assure market transparency so that investors can find a fair assessment of the financial assets they invest in. I am sure that they do their work in the best way possible, and, of course, the reputation of each agency is at stake with every rating that they prepare. They started to design their good and bad scales, trying to say how good or bad emissions are according to their own criteria. This is just one typical scale. Every rating agency will have its own, and it will have its reasons for supporting its own risk assessment as it is its value offer.

And all and all, we have to trust these agencies to do their work well, but in a way, there is always an embedded conflict of interest in this process. In many cases, agencies are paid by the

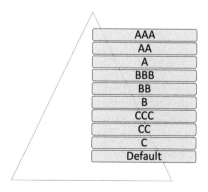

FIGURE 7.3 Example of a rating scale.

companies that they evaluate to issue their ratings. This puts trustworthiness on the side of the agency, and although we trust these agencies, it would be more transparent if we had an independent third party involved in this process to ensure no conflict of interest is ever occurring. This is not by any means a simple thing, and although it has been discussed in different places in the world, it is something we have not found a real solution for just yet.

WHY IS SUSTAINABILITY RELEVANT FOR BONDS?

But the exciting thing here is how do we incorporate ESG (environmental, social, and governance) factors in bonds? Mainly because in the case of other assets, i.e., stocks, the connection can be more direct because of ownership. Also, as we assess sustainability for a company, we could look at what kind of operation they have and so identify key elements, i.e., ESG factors. How do we assess sustainability for specific financial instruments? In the case of bonds, although you could use some of that as a proxy, it is also slightly different if it is not the company we are talking about. We are trying to evaluate a lending process, so we could perhaps start to assess the use of the proceeds. And that is the place to start. What are we doing with the money? It is an actual contractual obligation that we are trying to set. So, it is fair to understand it from a risk perspective, as it would have to also show somehow as a risk. And it does make sense as creditworthiness is typically evaluated for bonds, and all those ESG factors might have a direct or indirect incidence on the bond issuer's creditworthiness. And we will get there as we see some examples ahead.

ESG integration into bond investing is very relevant because much money also goes into fixed income as an asset category. That is the main reason why this is so relevant. In the case of green, social, sustainability, and other bonds, it will be important to assess different elements of the issuance, the use of proceeds, and the issuer. Some investment professionals have their own approaches, for example, Robeco,[4] an international asset manager from the Netherlands, has a score, the F Score (Zandbergen-Albers, 2018), that they designed to measure something like those ESG factors for bonds. In their approach, they assess five elements that are relevant for the assessment: business position, corporate strategy, ESG profile, financial performance, and corporate structure. I'm not very familiar with the actual methodology behind this because it is proprietary to this asset manager, but it is exciting to see how some asset managers come out with their implementations of how to do it for bonds because there's still much more to be developed in this area. See Figure 7.4 for relevant elements of the integration of ESG bonds.

If we want to assess ESG factors in bond valuation, we also need to measure credit risk elements, as GSS+ bonds are also built on the same legal structure as other bonds.

If we check the work of Prof. Caroline Flammer (Flammer, 2021), we find that green bonds, particularly corporate green bonds, are not so different from traditional bonds. Prof. Flammer also finds three relevant facts regarding corporate green bonds in her work

(i) corporate green bonds have become more prevalent over time, (ii) corporate green bonds are more prevalent in industries in which the environment is material to the firm's operations (e.g., energy), and (iii) corporate green bonds are especially prevalent in China, the US, and Europe.

FIGURE 7.4 What is relevant when integrating ESG into bonds?

But in a way, it is not that green bonds were intended to be better than other bonds. They are just somehow different. They do not look very different from traditional bonds because traditional bonds were already good enough as they were designed, and GSS+ bonds take the best of that. Traditional bonds were financial products that already had worked well; we just wanted to make them better by earmarking or labeling the use of the proceeds for specific sustainability purposes.

ISSUANCE OF BONDS

Debt issuance works just like lending money. It works in a very similar fashion. There are different elements to keep in mind when a bond is issued. If an issuer is willing to fund their activities, other questions will be asked. In essence, to better understand what characteristics the emission will have. Let us think of a general example to try to build a parallel. Imagine a friend of yours is asking for a loan from their local bank. Perhaps the banker already knows them as a client, but the banker will inquire about a couple of things; for starters: How is the business going? How many years have you been working there? How much is your income or salary? Are you married? Do you have any children? What do you need the money for? And perhaps several other things. In essence, that will be the same thing with countries and companies. They're just different kinds of institutions, and there is also the issue of scale. But in the end, they will undergo due diligence to determine their emission characteristics.

In the case of a company, you would question its profitability, leverage, intangibles, cost of capital, etc. All sorts of that can indicate their financial health; you can start to profile what kind of risk the company has. In the case of a country, it is a very similar thing; it's just bigger again. So, you would have to inquire about their external debt, liquidity, the balance of trade, etc. And, of course, that is because a country is way more complicated to analyze financially than a company. So, a company is much more complex to analyze financially than an individual.

In the case of GSS+ bonds, we also talk about the use of proceeds to identify what kind of bond we are talking about, i.e., green, social, sustainability, etc. But we will also have to determine a process to evaluate and allocate the projects that will be funded with those proceeds. Once the money is allocated, it will have to be managed to make sure it complies with whatever the bond is disclaiming to follow, but it will also have to be able to report on what is happening with those projects and the money invested in them. Reporting is not necessarily something desirable as it takes up resources, mainly time and effort, but it gives certainty to the investor that the objectives of the bond are being achieved, and so it helps ensure compliance.

FIGURE 7.5 The bond process (International Capital Market Association, 2021a).

As we can see in Figure 7.5, the use of proceeds is a main component in the issuance of a GSS+ bond. That will yield a full process of project evaluation and selection, for managing those proceeds, reporting upon those activities, and reinitiating the cycle for further financing.

DIFFERENT CATEGORIES OF BONDS

What makes up a green bond? What makes them social? What makes them sustainable or sustainability-linked? Or whatever color we can think of. We have mentioned that the use of proceeds is the most relevant part. In some cases, one may find that precisely it is the use of the proceeds that determines the actual category for a bond.

Nowadays, we hear a lot about different denominations or categories for bonds. Bonds come in all colors and shapes, and there is a compelling reason for that. In general, all green social and sustainability (GSS) bonds have gained much traction recently due to investors' increased interest in shifting their investments toward more sustainable alternatives, and bonds seem to be the perfect gateway for that. Some categories for GSS bonds include the above-mentioned, plus transition bonds and sustainability-linked bonds (SLBs). The above-mentioned categories can also be found in Figure 7.6, which arranges GSS+ bonds by categories.

The growth and value of different categories for the fixed-income market can also be observed in Figure 7.7:

Green bonds

Green bonds are defined by their greenness, which basically means that their use of proceeds will be reserved for environmental projects. The use of proceeds for green bonds must be something environmentally related; i.e., the emission of green bonds by a big IT company could be assigned to invest in further supporting their operation with renewable energy.

Green bonds are perhaps the best-known bonds in sustainability. At the time this text was written, there were regulations with regard to green bonds in the European Union, and the US Securities and Exchange Commission (SEC) was already discussing how to regulate green bonds and other similar financial instruments.

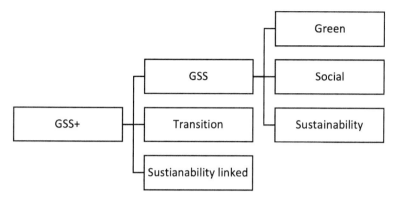

FIGURE 7.6 GSS+ categories of bonds.

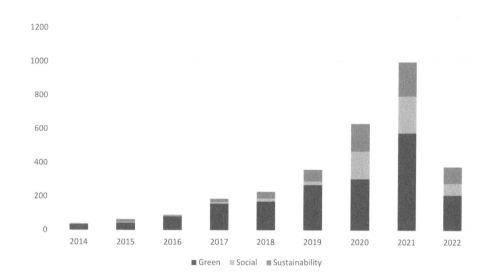

FIGURE 7.7 GSS+ issuance, sourced from Climate Bonds Initiative (2022).

According to the International Capital Market Association (ICMA), the eligible Green Projects categories, listed in no specific order, can include, but are not limited to, those shown in Figure 7.8:

The Green Bond Principles

The Green Bond Principles (GBP) are voluntary process guidelines that recommend transparency and disclosure and promote integrity in the development of the green bond market by clarifying the approach to the issuance of a green bond. These principles consider the following components and recommendations.

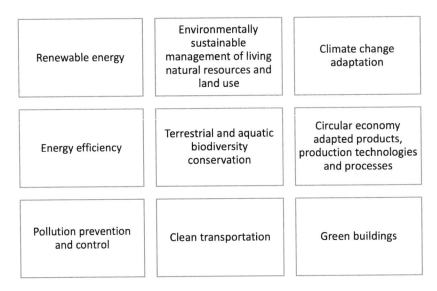

FIGURE 7.8 Eligible green bond project categories, based on International Capital Market Association (2021a).

The four core components for alignment with the GBP are:

1   Use of Proceeds
2   Process for Project Evaluation and Selection
3   Management of Proceeds
4   Reporting

The key recommendations for heightened transparency are:

1   Green Bond Frameworks
2   External Reviews

(International Capital Market Association, 2021a)

Green sovereign bonds

Green sovereign bonds are part of green bonds but deserve a special mention, as some countries have found an interesting opportunity to issue sovereign green bonds. Sovereign in this context means that bonds are issued by countries, i.e., France is a great example of a seasoned issuer that has learned the benefits of issuing green sovereign bonds, but many others, like Poland, for example, which is a little bit newer to this sort of emissions, have also found their way to this form of funding. In fact, many countries, not only in Europe but globally, have found this opportunity to be so attractive that they have become return-ing issuers of sovereign green bonds. For sovereign green bonds, government approvals are required before the actual process of targeting and identifying suitable projects. And in this

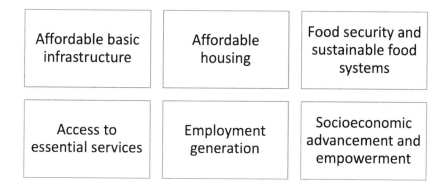

FIGURE 7.9 Eligible social bond project categories, based on International Capital Market Association (2021b).

case, reporting and verification will also be needed, as they are for other green bonds (Ando, Chenxu, Roch, & Wiriadinata, 2022).

Social bonds

Another popular category is social bonds. To qualify for a social bond, the proceeds must finance or refinance social projects or other activities that have positive social outcomes and address a social issue. In many cases, social projects are aimed at targeting populations below the poverty line, marginalized, migrant communities, unemployed women, sexual gender minorities, people with disabilities, and displaced persons.

According to the ICMA, social project categories include, but are not limited to, those shown in Figure 7.9:

The Social Bond Principles

The Social Bond Principles (SBP) are recommendations and guidelines that promote disclosure and integrity in advance of the social bond market. These principles support underwriters in facilitating transactions and preserving the integrity of the market.

The four core components for alignment with the SBP are:

1   Use of Proceeds
2   Process for Project Evaluation and Selection
3   Management of Proceeds
4   Reporting

The key recommendations for heightened transparency are:

1   Social Bond Frameworks
2   External Reviews

(International Capital Market Association, 2021b)

Sustainability bonds

Sustainability bonds are bond instruments for which the proceeds will be used to finance or refinance a combination of green and social projects.

The Sustainability bonds guidelines

Sustainability bonds are aligned with the four core components of both the GBP and the SBP. (International Capital Market Association, 2021c).

Sustainability-linked bonds

SLBs are another category that is also becoming popular, and they are connected to payments related to key performance indicators or (KPIs). If you have a background in business management, you may be familiar with this term. These KPIs trigger something; in this case, they provide incentives for the issuer to achieve their stated goals. The issuers of an SLB establish certain KPIs to explicitly commit to delivering the stated sustainability outcome within a certain timeframe. The issuer of the bond is usually incentivized by receiving a certain perk on the repayment of the instrument. SLBs are a very innovative form of fixed income and are not to be confused with sustainability bonds described above.

The Sustainability-Linked Bonds Principles

The Sustainability-Linked Bond Principles recommendations and guidelines profile best practices for financial instruments to incorporate ESG goals in their design. They aim to promote integrity in the development of the market.

The SLBs have five core components:

1　Selection of key performance indicators (KPI)
2　Calibration of Sustainability Performance Targets (SPTs)
3　Bond Characteristics
4　Reporting
5　Verification

(International Capital Market Association, 2020b)

Transition bonds

Transition bonds focus on an issuer's climate change-related commitments and practices, aligning with the Paris Agreement's ambitions. Capital markets have a key role in enabling the climate transition by ensuring financing from investors to issuers wishing to address climate-related risks and opportunities.

Climate Transition Finance Handbook

To facilitate the transition, the Climate Transition Finance Handbook provides guidance to capital market members on the practices, activities, and disclosures required for raising funds for climate transition-related instruments on the market.

According to the ICMA, there are two formats and key elements for this purpose:

(1) Use of Proceeds instruments, as defined in the GBP, SBP, and SBG
(2) General Corporate Purpose instruments aligned to the SLB principles

There are four key elements to these recommendations:

1 Issuer's climate transition strategy and governance
2 Business model environmental materiality
3 Climate transition strategy to be "science-based," including targets and pathways
4 Implementation transparency

(International Capital Market Association, 2020a)

OTHER RELEVANT BOND RESOURCES

The ICMA[5] and the Climate Bond Initiative (CBI)[6] are both great sources of information regarding GSS+ bonds. Further and more current information regarding bonds can usually be found on their websites.

SUSTAINABILITY-LINKED LOANS AND OTHER FORMS OF FINANCING

Although bonds are an important part of corporate and government funding, they cannot cover all needs. Usually, bond issuances go for bigger tickets, and so they leave opportunities for other forms of financing that have also thrived in sustainable finance (SF) in recent years. Sustainability-linked loans are also an important part of the debt market. Sustainability-linked loans are any type of loan instrument, including guarantee lines, letters of credit, bonding lines, etc., which incentivize a borrower to achieve pre-negotiated sustainability objectives. Categories for sustainability-linked loans (SLLs) include, but are not limited to, those shown in Figure 7.10:

Sustainability-linked loans principles (SLLPs)

Sustainability-linked loans are any type of loan instruments and/or contingent facilities (such as bonding lines, guarantee lines, or letters of credit) that incentivize the borrower's achievement of ambitious, predetermined sustainability performance objectives. The borrower's

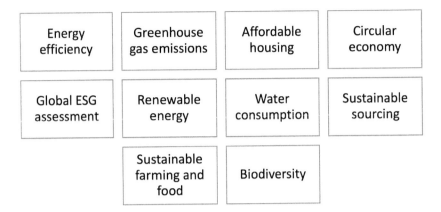

FIGURE 7.10 Common categories of targets for SLL, based on Loan Market Association (2019).

sustainability performance is measured using SPTs, which include KPIs, external ratings, and/or equivalent metrics and which measure improvements in the borrower's sustainability profile.

The SLLPs set out a framework that enables market participants to clearly understand the characteristics of an SLL described by four core components:

1   Relationship to Borrower's Overall Corporate Social Responsibility (CSR) Strategy
2   Target Setting – Measuring the Sustainability of the Borrower
3   Reporting
4   Review

(Loan Market Association, 2019)

IN A NUTSHELL

As we can see, some of these bond categories are nuances that come from the corporate and government sector allowing for the funding of sustainable projects. Some of these bond categories may appear to be more groundbreaking, as others simply earmark the use of proceeds for specific goals. In all cases, they seem to advance funding for much-needed causes, and the trends of the market show how increasing interest from the market exists for these categories. The actual intention to categorize them and increase their scope of investment, in the end, is to offer a wider set of alternatives for investors, and as we see these categories grow, more regulation is still evolving in different areas of the world.

Financial markets are going even faster than regulators to design and promote some categories of bonds and other forms of financing, and although clear regulation and taxonomies are needed, bond principles are certifications as well to provide certainty to all participants of the market. In addition to that, the bond principles and best practices help define a minimum standard for reporting and verification that is also needed. Fixed income is already a very successful area of SF, but we can expect more to come soon as it matures.

DISCUSSION QUESTIONS

1 Why is sustainability relevant for bonds?
2 What is the difference between stocks and bonds?
3 Are bonds considered more secure, as an investment, than other asset classes? Why?
4 What are government-issued bonds?
5 How are bonds valued?
6 What are green bonds? What types of projects can be funded by green bonds?
7 What is the purpose of social bonds? What types of projects can be funded by social bonds?
8 What are sustainability bonds? How are they different from green and social bonds?
9 What are sustainability-linked bonds (SLBs)?
10 What are transition bonds?

NOTES

1 In this text, we will define "traditional bonds" as all those bonds not considered in GSS+ categories.
2 The plus sign in GSS+ refers to others labels or categories of bonds that may include transition bonds, sustainability linked bonds, and others.
3 An IOU is signed document acknowledging a debt.
4 For further information, see https://www.robeco.com/en-int/
5 For further reference, see https://www.icmagroup.org/
6 For further reference, see https://www.climatebonds.net/

WORKS CITED

Ando, S., Chenxu, F., Roch, F., & Wiriadinata, U. (2022). *Sovereign climate debt instruments: An overview of the green and catastrophe bond markets.* International Monetary Fund.

Climate Bonds Initiative. (2022, H1). *Interactive data platform.* Retrieved from https://www.climatebonds.net/market/data/

Flammer, C. (2021). Corporate green bonds. *Journal of Financial Economics, 142*(2), 499–516.

International Capital Market Association. (2020a, December). *Climate transition finance handbook guidance for issuers.* Retrieved from https://www.icmagroup.org/assets/documents/Regulatory/Green-Bonds/Climate-Transition-Finance-Handbook-December-2020-091220.pdf

International Capital Market Association. (2020b, June). *Sustainability-linked bond principles voluntary process guidelines.* Retrieved from https://www.icmagroup.org/assets/documents/Regulatory/Green-Bonds/June-2020/Sustainability-Linked-Bond-Principles-June-2020-171120.pdf

International Capital Market Association. (2021a, June). *Green bond principles voluntary process guidelines for issuing green bonds.* Retrieved from https://www.icmagroup.org/assets/documents/Sustainable-finance/2022-updates/Green-Bond-Principles_June-2022-280622.pdf

International Capital Market Association. (2021b, June). *Social bond principles voluntary process guidelines for issuing social bonds.* Retrieved from https://www.icmagroup.org/assets/documents/Sustainable-finance/2022-updates/Social-Bond-Principles_June-2022v3-020822.pdf

International Capital Market Association. (2021c, June). *Sustainability bond guidelines.* Retrieved from https://www.icmagroup.org/assets/documents/Sustainable-finance/2021-updates/Sustainability-Bond-Guidelines-June-2021-140621.pdf

Loan Market Association. (2019, September 27). *Sustainability linked loan principles.* Retrieved from https://www.icmagroup.org/assets/documents/Regulatory/Green-Bonds/LMASustainabilityLinkedLoan-Principles-270919.pdf

Zandbergen-Albers, M. (2018, July 15). *Fact or fiction: SI only works with equities.* Retrieved from https://www.robeco.com/uk/insights/2018/07/fact-or-fiction-si-only-works-with-equities.html

CHAPTER 8

Indices and passive investments

WHAT IS AN INDEX?

Indices are a common topic in finance. They are designed to represent the market, track it, or for any other practical purpose. Passive investments (Easley, Michayluk, O'Hara, & Putniņš, 2021) are investment strategies commonly deploying those indices to optimize their operation. Indices are a trendy topic, as we hear about them frequently in the media, and they are the easiest way to access diversification. Indices come in different shapes and sizes, and they serve varied objectives. They are designed to cater to different audiences and are created around various themes. The general idea behind indices is to have a reference or benchmark to use for investments and design passive investment strategies. Indices can also represent how the market is doing at a certain point in time, and those are the indices we hear about, i.e., "the Dow Jones (Wikipedia, 2023a) was going up or down," or "the S&P500 (Wikipedia, 2023b) registered a record high." Passive investments are investment strategies that aim to obtain returns with little to no stock trading during the investment period – index investing is one form of passive investing.

WHAT IS A SUSTAINABILITY INDEX?

Sustainability indices are the same as traditional indices, but they also incorporate elements of sustainability. They serve as a reference point for investors and a benchmark for sustainability-themed investment funds and exchange traded funds (ETFs) (Investopedia, 2022). They have registered significant growth in interest in recent years. An ETF is a category of pooled investment securities. ETFs can track indices, commodities, assets, investment strategies, etc. ETFs are very similar to mutual funds, but unlike them, ETFs can be traded on a stock exchange.

ETFs are a growing asset class. And since not all regulation is there yet, at least in some geographies, it is crucial to be cautious to distinguish genuine efforts toward sustainability from not so humble attempts to avoid greenwashing. Yet again, new advances in taxonomies for green funds exist and will continue to evolve everywhere, but we must still exercise caution. We must agree on what sustainable finance (SF) is in funds and define it at the regulatory level. In other words, a taxonomy for green funds is needed. And until we reach that point, it is on the side of the investors and financial institutions to preserve the integrity of SF in passive investments and index investments.

DOI: 10.4324/9781003274735-8

TABLE 8.1 Key differences between mutual funds and ETFs

Characteristic	Description
Fees	Mutual funds typically have higher fees and expenses than ETFs due in part to the costs of active management and trading. ETFs generally have lower expenses, but investors may incur trading commissions when buying or selling shares.
Minimum investment	Mutual funds may require a minimum investment amount, while ETFs can be purchased in any amount.
Tax efficiency	ETFs may be more tax-efficient than mutual funds due to their structure, which allows for more flexibility in managing capital gains and losses.

In Europe, there is already significant advance through these regulatory efforts, particularly in those countries that are part of the European Union and Switzerland that have already advanced in regulatory efforts to define the criteria for "green" in funds and to prevent greenwashing.

Mutual funds and ETFs: The package deals

Both mutual funds and ETFs are types of investment vehicles that allow investors to pool their money together to invest in a diversified portfolio of stocks, bonds, or other assets (Elton, Gruber, & De Souza, 2019). They can both be considered passive investments, but there are some key differences between the two. Both mutual funds and ETFs can be useful tools for investors looking to build a diversified portfolio of investments, and the choice between the two will depend on an investor's specific needs and preferences (Wikipedia, 2022). Some of these differences can be observed in Table 8.1.

WHY ARE SUSTAINABILITY INDICES IMPORTANT?

Sustainability in indices helps benchmark alternatives for investments. Investors take indices as a reference point to check who is who in relevant topics, i.e., sustainability. They also simplify how people can assess what kind of sustainability they want by themes, i.e., water, human rights, equality, biodiversity, etc. The list is so long it cannot be exhaustive.

Not all sustainability indices have been utterly credible in the past, so it is essential to review what and who is behind each of them and what the aim is for a particular index to attain. And what kind of criteria or principles are used for designing them. "ESG is simply another way of measuring the centuries-old concept of socially responsible investing" (Makridis & Fotsch, 2023).

INDICES HELP BUILD A REPUTATION

Indices create awareness of the reputation of the companies that become part of an index. It is one of their most relevant characteristics. Indices help build a reputation, i.e., the most sustainable companies in the world would like to be part of the Dow Jones World Sustainability Index. Being part of a recognized index is a clear statement.

As indices serve as benchmarks for mutual funds and ETFs, once a company is included in the index, funds that track the index typically must rebalance their holdings to replicate that inclusion. Being part of the index creates a reputation and helps to drive new cashflows and interest toward the company. Sustainability indices also help build credibility as the companies they choose to include in the index will be the most relevant in their industry or sustainability efforts.

DIFFERENT TYPES OF INDICES

Indices can also be sector, asset, or geographically specific. Sometimes they can also represent several categories simultaneously and be as clear as the needs of their stakeholders. Those stakeholders include investment institutions, stock exchanges, investors, the media, and anybody. ESG (environmental, social, and governance) research vendors also try to integrate part of the information contained in the indices. Some are even very closely related to how those indices were designed. For example, in the case of RobecoSAM and Dow Jones, they jointly created the Dow Jones World Sustainability Index (S&P Dow Jones Indices, 2023). And as explained before, indices can also represent investment strategies.

WHO CREATES INDICES?

Data providers for indices include those well-known institutions mentioned above, such as S&P and Dow Jones, and others, such as Morningstar, Sustainalytics, Bloomberg, etc. Those data providers may even play different roles in procuring, analyzing, marketing, managing, and distributing information.

Sustainability indices are also an efficient way to diversify. So funds that track those indices can outsource the portfolio's design to reduce costs and offer reduced fees to their clients. And this is another exciting advantage. Passive funds are usually cost-effective for investors as they do not need to do much on the back to offer a diversified portfolio that may even portray a particular theme. You may still need a couple of analysts to work with the fund to keep on rebalancing as the benchmark changes, but that is not too complicated to do.

HOW MUCH DO INDICES CHANGE?

In a given year, indices can have several inclusions or deletions. If we consider an index with a certain number of items comprising them, we could expect some to change over time. As a real-life example, years ago, a prominent index company saw up to 29.5% annual component changes on average, including additions and deletions. In this case anonymity prevails as this is just for illustration's context. But as we can see, there could be significant changes in a given year for a given index. The components of an index are not carved in stone, meaning they are not permanent or completely stable. And there is a reason for that. Indices are expected to reflect a particular dynamic. As companies become relevant to the theme of reference or their trading volume changes, they might be more attractive as an index component. Several companies are usually listed in an index. That number is determined by operating the index and is not fixed either. Whoever designs an index considers the chosen number of elements representative enough to describe what they want to show. However, companies go in and companies go out of that index. Of course, more established indices might not have as much movement in the long run.

WHY IS IT IMPORTANT TO TRACK THOSE CHANGES?

When you track an index, we can also see its evolution and how much value it creates. For example, if we checked the Dow Jones Industrial Average Index (DJIA) or the SP500 on any given day, we would know their value on a point scale. That scale reflects the accumulated value over time for that index. In the case of most indices, it is an aggregated value of several companies that were chosen to be part of the index during a specific time. And those companies are believed to be representative of the market.

However, it is only a representation and not the whole market, and there are different reasons. On one side, some indices have been tracking companies for decades. They used to follow specific companies to simplify index calculation when calculations and data processing were much more rudimentary than what we have today. That has changed radically; we have enough processing capacity to deal with more information. Today we can even track every company in the market in real time; it would just be too much work. It is possible to do this if need be, but there is no point in updating every single company in the market into an index, as some companies might not even be relevant. And some may be creating noise rather than helping explain the market dynamic.

An index is intended to be representative. We choose the most relevant companies to be part of the index. We also believe that the information that tracks those companies is also relevant, and that is part of the value added that indices offer. The more tracking, the more time and money it would take to process the index, so it is also a practical matter. And that also goes for industries, as not every company in an index will be tracked, just the most representative.

TAILOR-MADE INDICES

Regarding processing capacity, we nowadays have much more than we had decades ago when indices started to thrive. We can now design our investments to track any aspect of sustainability that we can relate to. Indices can be as specific or individual as investors want them to be. They can be tailor-made or custom-made. Different asset managers now offer the possibility of choosing an investment portfolio that follows concrete goals and ESG criteria, unique strategies, or even AI solutions to better target preferences or needs. It is part of the evolution of how it can be done; the options are enormous, perhaps unlimited, with the current level of technology that we have today. We can only expect this to evolve as passive investments are essential to the investment universe. In an easy, usually inexpensive fashion, we can expect to get more creative alternatives for assigning our assets. And that convenience and cost efficiency is the most crucial strength of passive investments for end-users and investors.

IN A NUTSHELL

As these and other topics of SF continue to evolve and thrive, investors continue to have the responsibility to do their homework regarding them, in other words, to run due diligence on their investments or their clients' investments in the case of financial advisors. As AI continues to bloom and offers more sophisticated and clear-cut solutions for assets, more opaque processes seem to come from the investor side. Investors are responsible for their holdings, whether they take advice from third parties or machines, and this will not change. The investments they make by choosing their advisors and strategies matter. Passive investments seem to widen the gap between investors and their investments, but still, much information is typically available and publicly disclosed regarding investments and should be analyzed. This means that the ultimate responsibility of the investment choice ultimately falls on the investor.

DISCUSSION QUESTIONS

1 What are indices and what are they used for?
2 What are passive investments, and how are indices used in them?
3 What is a sustainability index, and how is it different from traditional indices?
4 What are ETFs, and how are they related to indices?
5 What is greenwashing, and why is it a concern in passive investments?
6 How is regulation addressing the issue of greenwashing in passive investments?
7 What are mutual funds and ETFs, and what are the key differences between them?
8 Why are sustainability indices important?
9 What is the relationship between sustainability indices and a company's reputation?
10 What are some different types of indices, and who are their stakeholders?

WORKS CITED

Easley, D., Michayluk, D., O'Hara, M., & Putniņš, T. J. (2021). The active world of passive investing. *Review of Finance, 25*(5), 1433–1471.

Elton, E. J., Gruber, M. J., & De Souza, A. (2019). Passive mutual funds and ETFs: Performance and comparison. *Journal of Banking & Finance, 106*, 265–275.

Investopedia. (2022). *Exchange-traded funds (ETF) explanation with pros and cons.* Retrieved from https://www.investopedia.com/terms/e/etf.asp

Makridis, C., & Fotsch, B. (2023, February 02). *Fast company*. Retrieved February 2022, from ESG investors have good intentions, but there's a better way to measure corporate impact and health: https://www.fastcompany.com/90844629/esg-investors-better-way-to-measure-corporate-impact

S&P Dow Jones Indices. (2023). *Dow Jones Sustainability World Index*. Retrieved from https://www.spglobal.com/spdji/en/indices/esg/dow-jones-sustainability-world-index/#overview

Wikipedia. (2022, March). *ETF vs. Mutual Fund: What's the difference?* Retrieved March 2023, from https://www.investopedia.com/articles/investing/110314/key-differences-between-etfs-and-mutual-funds.asp

Wikipedia. (2023a). *Dow Jones Industrial Average*. Retrieved from https://en.wikipedia.org/wiki/Dow_Jones_Industrial_Average

Wikipedia. (2023b). *S&P 500*. Retrieved from https://en.wikipedia.org/wiki/S%26P_500

CHAPTER 9

Alternative assets

WHAT ARE ALTERNATIVE ASSETS?

Alternative assets are investments that fall outside of traditional investment categories like equity stocks, bonds, and cash. They are typically less liquid and more complex than traditional assets and may require specialized knowledge and expertise to manage effectively. Alternative assets can include a wide range of investment types, such as the ones in Figure 9.1.

- Real estate (RE) investments in physical properties like commercial and residential RE, as well as real estate investment trusts (REITs).
- Private equity (PE) refers to investments in privately held companies that are not publicly traded on a stock exchange.
- Hedge funds are investment vehicles that pool money from multiple investors and use a variety of strategies to generate returns.
- Commodities include investments in physical assets like gold, silver, oil, and agricultural products.
- Infrastructure is investments in large-scale projects like toll roads, airports, and water treatment plants.
- Art and collectibles are investments in unique items like artwork, antique furniture, and rare coins.

Alternative assets can provide investors with diversification benefits and potentially higher returns than traditional assets. However, they are also typically riskier and may be subject to greater volatility and liquidity concerns. As such, alternative assets are generally considered suitable only for sophisticated and experienced investors who have the expertise to evaluate and manage the risks involved.

KEY CHALLENGES

There are several challenges to effectively integrating ESG (environmental, social, and governance) considerations into investment decision-making. One such challenge is the need to harmonize metrics across different ESG factors to enable consistent and comparable

DOI: 10.4324/9781003274735-9

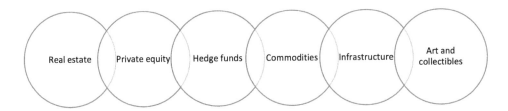

FIGURE 9.1 Some examples of alternative asset investment categories.

assessments. Additionally, the disclosure of ESG-related information by companies is important to ensure transparency and accountability.

For firms, there is a need to identify and assess the materiality of ESG factors in their business operations and to develop strategies for addressing them. Institutional investors face challenges in identifying which ESG factors are most relevant to their investment strategies and in determining how to integrate this information into their decision-making processes.

Another key challenge is the inclusion of climate risks in all asset classes, including equities, fixed income, and alternative investments. This requires the development of new and better benchmarks to assess the exposure of investments to climate-related risks. Finally, there is a need to increase efforts to internalize ESG-related costs, which involves ensuring that companies are held responsible for the negative externalities associated with their operations.

SOME RELEVANT CATEGORIES OF ALTERNATIVE ASSETS

As alternative assets are investments that fall outside of traditional investment, a lot of things can fit the description. As we cannot get a comprehensive list, some relevant examples of alternative assets that are also relevant to sustainable finance (SF) are included below.

Real estate

RE is a popular alternative asset investment in SF due to its potential for long-term financial returns and its ability to create positive environmental and social impacts. Sustainable RE investments aim to reduce energy consumption, carbon emissions, and waste generation while also promoting social inclusion and resilience. Sustainable RE projects can take many forms, including green buildings, sustainable communities, and affordable housing developments. These investments not only contribute to the development of sustainable infrastructure but also align with the United Nations' Sustainable Development Goals, particularly SDG 11, which calls for investment in sustainable cities and communities. Overall, investing in sustainable RE can generate significant positive impacts on society and the environment while also providing financial returns to investors.

Commodities

Commodities, such as gold, oil, and agricultural products, have become an increasingly popular alternative asset investment in SF. Sustainable commodity investments focus on promoting environmentally responsible practices in the production, distribution, and consumption of commodities. This includes investing in sustainable agriculture, renewable energy, and responsible mining practices. Sustainable commodity investments also take into account the social and economic impacts of commodity production, such as supporting small-scale farmers and indigenous communities. By investing in sustainable commodities, investors can promote responsible resource management, reduce environmental degradation, and support sustainable development. Moreover, sustainable commodity investments can offer diversification benefits and potentially high returns to investors. Overall, investing in sustainable commodities can create positive impacts on society and the environment while also providing financial returns to investors.

Private equity

PE refers to investments made in private companies or non-publicly traded assets, such as RE or infrastructure. PE has become an increasingly popular alternative asset investment in SF as it offers the potential for high returns and the ability to create positive environmental and social impacts. Sustainable PE investments focus on supporting companies that promote environmental sustainability, social inclusion, and corporate governance. This includes investing in companies that develop renewable energy, promote sustainable agriculture, or improve access to healthcare and education. Sustainable PE investments also consider the social and environmental impacts of a company's operations, such as reducing carbon emissions, promoting diversity and inclusion, and upholding human rights. By investing in sustainable PE, investors can contribute to sustainable development while also potentially achieving attractive financial returns. Overall, sustainable PE investments can create significant positive impacts on society and the environment while also providing financial returns to investors.

Hedge funds

Hedge funds are a type of alternative asset investment that has gained interest in SF due to their potential for high returns and their ability to support sustainable development. Sustainable hedge funds invest in companies that promote environmental sustainability, social responsibility, and corporate governance. This includes investing in companies that develop clean technologies, promote sustainable agriculture, or improve access to healthcare and education. Sustainable hedge funds also consider the social and environmental impacts of a company's operations, such as reducing carbon emissions, promoting diversity and inclusion, and upholding human rights.

Infrastructure

Infrastructure refers to the essential physical and organizational structures and facilities that are necessary for the operation of a society or enterprise. It includes roads, bridges, airports, water supply, and sewage systems. Infrastructure as an alternative asset investment has gained traction in SF to address the global infrastructure gap and promote sustainable development. Sustainable infrastructure investments focus on projects that generate positive social, environmental, and economic impacts while also providing long-term financial returns to investors. These investments contribute to the development of resilient and sustainable infrastructure.

Arts and collectibles

Arts and collectibles, such as paintings, sculptures, etc., have been increasingly recognized as an alternative asset investment in SF. Collectors and investors are drawn to these assets because they offer diversification and the potential for high returns. Moreover, investing in art and collectibles can contribute to sustainable development by preserving cultural heritage and promoting creativity. Sustainable art investments focus on artworks that are socially responsible, ecologically conscious, and culturally significant. This includes investing in artworks that reflect the diversity, address social issues, and support sustainable practices. Sustainable collectors and investors also consider the environmental impact of their investments, including the materials and processes used to create the artwork.

RISK

Alternative asset investments can help hedge investment risk by providing diversification benefits to an investment portfolio. Alternative assets, such as RE, commodities, PE, and hedge funds, have a low correlation with traditional asset classes, such as stocks and bonds. This means that alternative assets can perform differently from traditional assets in various market conditions, which can help to reduce overall portfolio risk. Additionally, alternative asset investments typically have lower liquidity than traditional investments, which can discourage investors from selling off their investments during periods of market volatility. This can help to prevent panic selling and provide a more stable return profile for the overall portfolio. By including alternative assets in an investment portfolio, investors can potentially improve risk-adjusted returns and achieve a more balanced and diversified investment strategy.

SIX PRINCIPLES OF RESPONSIBLE INVESTMENT

The six principles of responsible investment (PRI) are a set of guidelines that investors can follow to incorporate ESG issues into their investment strategies (PRI Association, 2023). More on the principles can be seen in Figure 9.2.

The first principle emphasizes the importance of considering ESG issues in the investment analysis and decision-making process. This involves assessing the impact of ESG factors on the long-term financial performance of investments.

The second principle encourages investors to be active owners and incorporate ESG issues into their ownership policies and practices. This involves engaging with companies to encourage better ESG performance and using voting rights to effect positive change.

The third principle stresses the need for appropriate disclosure of ESG issues by companies in which investments are made. This enables investors to make informed decisions and hold companies accountable for their ESG performance.

The fourth principle calls for the promotion of acceptance and implementation of the principles within the investment industry. This involves collaboration between investors, regulators, and other stakeholders to advance responsible investment practices.

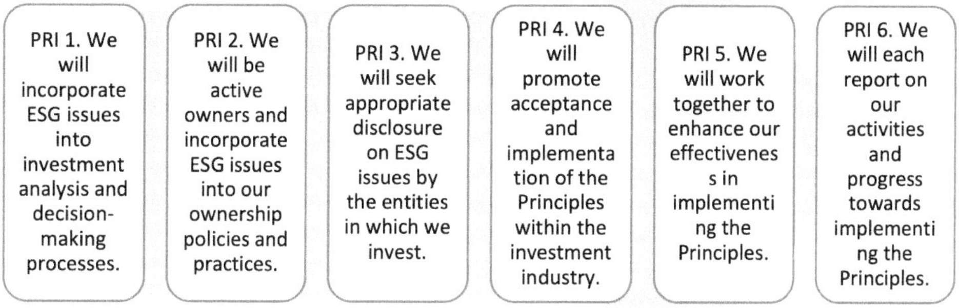

| PRI 1. We will incorporate ESG issues into investment analysis and decision-making processes. | PRI 2. We will be active owners and incorporate ESG issues into our ownership policies and practices. | PRI 3. We will seek appropriate disclosure on ESG issues by the entities in which we invest. | PRI 4. We will promote acceptance and implementation of the Principles within the investment industry. | PRI 5. We will work together to enhance our effectiveness in implementing the Principles. | PRI 6. We will each report on our activities and progress towards implementing the Principles. |

FIGURE 9.2 Six principles of responsible investment (PRI Association, 2023).

The fifth principle focuses on working together to enhance the effectiveness of implementing the principles. This involves sharing knowledge, resources, and best practices to advance responsible investment.

The sixth principle requires each investor to report on their activities and progress toward implementing the principles. This promotes transparency and accountability and enables stakeholders to evaluate the effectiveness of responsible investment practices.

IN A NUTSHELL

Alternative assets are investments that fall outside traditional investment categories and can provide diversification benefits and potentially higher returns than traditional assets. However, they are riskier and may require specialized knowledge to manage effectively. The integration of ESG criteria can help anticipate and reduce risks before they cause losses or costs, and PE investors have inherent corporate governance advantages compared to their public market peers.

The categories of alternative assets, have attractive returns, low correlation with other asset classes, and competitive advantages due to high market entry barriers. However, there are key challenges to consider, such as harmonization of metrics, disclosure, and inclusion of climate risks in all asset classes. The increasing efforts needed to achieve the internalization of ESG-related costs are crucial for sustainability in finance.

DISCUSSION QUESTIONS

1 What are alternative assets?
2 What are some of the alternative asset categories, and what are some examples of specific investments within each category?
3 What are the benefits of investing in alternative assets?
4 What are the risks associated with investing in alternative assets?
5 Who are the ideal investors for alternative assets?
6 What is the importance of considering ESG criteria in financial decision-making?
7 What are the key challenges associated with integrating ESG factors into alternative assets?
8 How can PE investors use ESG factors to enhance investment returns?
9 What are the different types of PE investments?
10 What are some of the key challenges facing the integration of environmental, social, and governance (ESG) factors when investing in alternative assets, and what are some potential solutions to these challenges?

WORKS CITED

PRI Association. (2023). *What are the Principles for Responsible Investment?* Retrieved from https://www.unpri.org/about-us/what-are-the-principles-for-responsible-investment

CHAPTER 10

Insurance and risk

INSURANCE

When talking about risk, we need to talk about insurance. Precisely because risk can never be avoided completely, but it can be reduced, managed, and/or redistributed (Keil, Cule, Lyytinen, & Schmidt, 1998). For example, even if you do not get out of your house, you are completely careful, it is not probable, but you can still have an accident inside your house. In that case, you may be trying to reduce risk to a minimum, but it does not mean you can avoid all risks. There is always going to be a certain amount of risk. So, why do we have insurance? We can distribute the cost of our risk to a third party because we can manage that risk better with the help of a professional that is in the business of managing risk.

Insurance is a contract between an individual or entity (the policyholder) and an insurance company (Chondrogiannis, Andronikou, Karanastasis, Litke, & Varvarigou, 2022) where the policyholder pays a premium in exchange for protection against potential future losses or damages. The insurance company agrees to compensate the policyholder for covered losses, such as damage to property, illness or injury, or liability arising from certain events or circumstances. Insurance provides a way for individuals and businesses to manage risk and protect themselves financially from unexpected events that could otherwise cause significant financial harm.

How do insurance companies work?

Individuals typically confront different levels of risk in their lives and day-to-day activities. Insurance companies understand that and offer coverage packages or policies to cover those risks regarding those individuals' driving, life, health, etc. Insurance companies pool a good number of clients and build a portfolio of policies. They try to profile those clients to understand their statistical risks and overall needs. Those clients, in general, will tend to be unique. This means that different individuals might have different needs, different risk levels, and different characteristics. The insurance company can design a model to set a price for each of those individuals to offset their risk exposure. This is determined by the available information that the insurance company has, and so they can be exposed to information asymmetry (Auronen, 2003).

Insurance companies make money by charging rates to their clients, but they also have to keep reserves to cover their obligations in case of contingencies. This is required by law and is in the best interest of their clients, but it adds to their costs. Insurance companies can only

DOI: 10.4324/9781003274735-10

do so much to manage their risk exposure, and sometimes they need to get insurance coverage themselves. Reinsurance companies provide this coverage on a larger scale, which helps to redistribute risk across different geographies.

Reinsurance

Reinsurance is a type of insurance that insurance companies use to transfer some of the risks they have assumed from their policyholders to another insurance company. In other words, reinsurance is insurance for insurers. Insurance companies buy reinsurance policies to protect themselves from catastrophic losses or to reduce their exposure to risk. Reinsurers assume some or all of the risks that the insurance company has underwritten, and, in exchange, the insurance company pays a premium to the reinsurer. Reinsurance allows insurers to spread their risks over a wider geographic area and diversify their portfolios, which can help them manage their exposure to large and unexpected losses (Patrik, 2006).

WHAT IS RISK?

Financial risk refers to the potential for financial loss or uncertainty in achieving financial goals due to market volatility, economic conditions, or other factors. Financial risk can arise from a variety of sources, including investment risks, credit risks, liquidity risks, and operational risks. To manage financial risk, individuals and organizations can take a number of steps, including:

Diversification: Spreading investments across different asset classes, sectors, and geographic regions can help reduce the impact of market volatility and specific risks.

Risk assessment: Assessing the level of risk associated with different investments or financial decisions can help individuals and organizations make informed choices about how to allocate their resources.

Risk management strategies: Developing strategies for managing risk, such as setting stop-loss limits, hedging against potential losses, or implementing asset allocation models, can help reduce exposure to potential losses.

Monitoring and adjusting: Regularly monitoring investments and financial decisions, and making adjustments as needed based on changing market conditions or risk levels, can help individuals and organizations stay on track toward their financial goals.

Professional advice: Seeking advice from financial professionals, such as financial advisors, can help individuals and organizations make informed decisions about managing financial risk.

Managing financial risk is an ongoing process and requires a combination of education, discipline, and a willingness to adapt to changing market conditions. By taking steps to manage financial risk, individuals and organizations can help protect themselves against potential losses and achieve their financial goals over the long term.

DIFFERENT KINDS OF RISK

There are different kinds of risks that insurance can cover. For the purpose of our topic, transitional and physical risk would be relevant, but other sorts of risk are also important, such as:

traditional risk, catastrophic risk, environmental risk, etc. Traditional risk is the one that results from common activities, i.e., suffering an accident while walking on the street.

Physical risk

Physical risk refers to the potential harm or damage that can arise from natural disasters, accidents, and other physical events. These events can include floods, earthquakes, hurricanes, fires, and other similar incidents. Physical risk can affect individuals, businesses, and communities, causing financial losses, property damage, and even loss of life. The impact of physical risk can be reduced through measures such as risk management, disaster preparedness, and insurance (Wiklund, 2021).

Transition risk

Transition risk refers to the financial risks that companies, industries, and economies may face as they transition to a low-carbon economy. This type of risk is caused by changes in policy, technology, market, and consumer behavior that can impact the value of assets or lead to increased costs or financial losses. For example, a shift toward renewable energy sources could lead to a decline in demand for fossil fuels and associated infrastructure, which could result in stranded assets and loss of revenue for companies that rely on these industries. Companies that fail to manage transition risks effectively may face credit downgrades, increased borrowing costs, and potential legal liabilities (Semieniuk, Campiglio, Mercure, Volz, & Edwards, 2021).

CLIMATE-CHANGE-RELATED RISK

Climate change has become a significant concern for the insurance industry due to its potential impact on various natural catastrophes. The following are some of the risk elements associated with climate change that pose significant challenges for insurers, as seen in Figure 10.1.

Mitigation and adaptation

Mitigation and adaptation are two complementary strategies used to address the impacts of climate change. While mitigation aims to reduce greenhouse gas emissions and limit the extent of climate change, adaptation focuses on building resilience to the changes that are already occurring (Stehr & Von Storch, 2005).

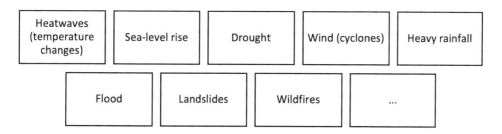

FIGURE 10.1 Risk elements associated with climate change.

Mitigation involves actions that aim to reduce or avoid greenhouse gas emissions in order to mitigate climate change. This can include measures such as transitioning to renewable energy sources, increasing energy efficiency, and improving transportation infrastructure to reduce carbon emissions. Mitigation efforts can also include afforestation and reforestation to capture and store carbon in trees and soils.

Adaptation, on the other hand, involves actions that aim to reduce the risks and impacts of climate change that are already occurring. This can include measures such as improving water management practices to cope with drought and flooding, designing buildings and infrastructure to withstand extreme weather events, and enhancing natural ecosystems to provide climate resilience.

Both mitigation and adaptation are necessary to address the risks of climate change, and insurers have an important role to play in supporting these efforts. Insurance companies can incentivize mitigation measures by offering lower premiums for policyholders who take steps to reduce their carbon footprint, such as installing solar panels or using energy-efficient appliances. Insurers can also support adaptation measures by providing coverage for climate risks and offering risk management services to help policyholders prepare for and respond to extreme weather events.

Catastrophe modeling

Catastrophe modeling is a method used by insurance companies, financial institutions, and other organizations to assess and manage the risks associated with natural and man-made disasters. It involves using computer models and simulations to estimate the potential losses that could be incurred in the event of a catastrophic event such as a hurricane, earthquake, terrorist attack, or pandemic.

Catastrophe models take into account various factors, such as the physical characteristics of the event, the location and vulnerability of the assets, and the potential economic and social impacts of the disaster. They use historical data, scientific research, and other sources of information to create a range of scenarios and probabilities for different types of catastrophes.

Insurance companies use catastrophe modeling to price their policies and to estimate their exposure to catastrophic losses. Financial institutions use it to manage their risk and to assess the potential impact of catastrophic events on their investments. Government agencies and emergency responders use it to plan for and respond to disasters.

ENVIRONMENTAL RISK

Environmental risk refers to the potential for harm to human health or the natural environment due to exposure to hazardous substances, conditions, or events such as pollution, climate change, or natural disasters. Environmental risks can have significant impacts on public health, ecosystems, and the economy. Some examples can be seen in Figure 10.2.

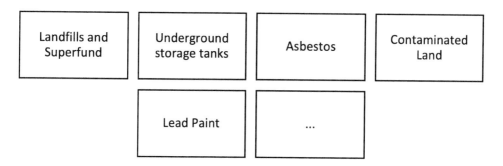

FIGURE 10.2 Examples of environmental risk.

EXTERNALITIES: WHO IS PAYING FOR ALL OF THIS?

Natural catastrophes are a major concern, especially in less developed countries, where they cause the most damage. Asia has seen many of these catastrophes, which have cost many lives. Europe and South America are better equipped to deal with such events, while the United States and Canada have significant losses but benefit from insurance payouts, which inject money into the economy. This perverse incentive is because we do not account for the value lost, only money gained. Artificial losses are shown in green, and as we continue to damage the environment, we expect more weather events to increase. The United States is more prepared to deal with these events due to insurance, but we should focus on preventing environmental damage instead.

Oil spills

Regarding oil spills, the insurance company would assess the assets and liabilities of the policy-holder for the oil spill liabilities. For example, in the Deepwater Horizon case, the insurance company would assess the total cost of the oil spill and determine how much of that liability would be covered by the policyholder's insurance policy.

Insurance companies have a liability to cover the costs of an oil spill. However, it's impossible to completely clean up the effects of an oil spill. The insurance company will pay for all the liability, but only up to the point that coverage runs out or if the company goes bankrupt. We shouldn't make decisions beyond our means and should take a conservative approach. Double tankers are a technology that could prevent most, if not all, oil spills, but they are not the first choice for oil companies because they are more expensive. Insurance policies will cover some of the costs, but not everything, and determining who is responsible for how much is a costly and complicated process. To receive compensation, you may need to sue the company or insurance company, which is also a barrier. Ideally, those affected by an oil spill should receive automatic compensation, but this is not always the case.

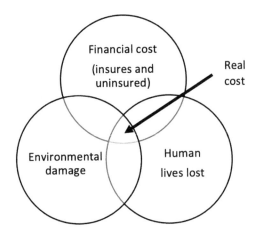

FIGURE 10.3 Real cost of environmental catastrophes.

Events, human, and economic cost

Climate disasters can have high human and economic costs, and these costs are often unevenly distributed. Understanding the ways in which different communities and regions are impacted can help policymakers develop strategies to reduce vulnerability and build resilience to climate disasters. Sometimes this cost is not even so evident, as can be seen in Figure 10.3.

In 2022, there were ten climate-fueled extreme weather events that caused more than US$3 billion worth of damage each. But the balance between economic and human costs can be very uneven, i.e., the Pakistan floods were the sixth most expensive event on the list, but also the disaster with the highest human cost, *The Guardian* pointed out. The flooding killed 1,739 people and displaced seven million (World Economic Forum, 2023).

Climate disasters such as floods, droughts, hurricanes, and wildfires can have significant and long-lasting impacts on human and economic systems. The costs of these disasters are often unevenly distributed, affecting certain communities and regions more severely than others. Here are some reasons why the human and economic costs of climate disasters can be unevenly distributed:

Geographical location: Climate disasters tend to affect some regions more severely than others. For example, coastal communities are more vulnerable to hurricanes and flooding, while inland areas are more vulnerable to droughts and wildfires. This can result in uneven economic impacts, as regions that are heavily reliant on certain industries, such as agriculture or tourism, may be hit harder than others.

Socioeconomic status: Climate disasters can exacerbate existing inequalities and disproportionately affect low-income communities. These communities often lack access to resources and infrastructure that can help them prepare for and recover from disasters. For example, they may have less access to insurance, emergency services, and evacuation routes, leaving them more vulnerable to the impacts of climate disasters.

Health: Climate disasters can have significant impacts on human health, particularly for vulnerable populations such as the elderly, children, and people with preexisting health conditions. For example, heat waves can cause heat exhaustion and heat stroke, while flooding can increase the risk of waterborne illnesses. These health impacts can be unevenly distributed based on factors such as age, income, and access to healthcare. The COVID-19 pandemic is another alarming example of this.

Infrastructure: Climate disasters can damage infrastructure such as roads, bridges, and buildings, which can have economic impacts on the affected communities. However, the cost of repairing and rebuilding infrastructure can also be unevenly distributed. Wealthier communities may have more resources to repair their infrastructure, while low-income communities may struggle to access the funds needed to rebuild.

Insured and uninsured losses

Insured losses are those losses that are covered by an insurance policy. When an individual or organization purchases an insurance policy, they pay a premium in exchange for the insurer assuming the financial risk of certain types of losses. If a covered loss event occurs, the policyholder can make a claim to the insurance company to receive compensation for the damages or losses suffered. Examples of insured losses include damages caused by a covered natural disaster, theft, etc.

Uninsured losses are those losses that are not covered by an insurance policy. This means that the individual or organization affected by the loss event is responsible for bearing the financial burden of the damages or losses suffered. Examples of uninsured losses include damages caused by certain natural disasters that are not covered by standard insurance policies, such as floods or earthquakes, etc.

Uninsured losses can pose a significant financial burden on individuals and organizations, particularly in the case of large-scale disasters. In some cases, governments may provide financial assistance to individuals and businesses affected by uninsured losses, but this is not always the case.

INNOVATION IN INSURANCE

Significant advances have been created in insurance in recent years, i.e., microinsurance and parametric insurance.

Microinsurance

Microinsurance is a type of insurance that is designed to provide coverage to low-income individuals, families, and small businesses in developing countries or other financially underserved communities. It is typically characterized by low premiums, small coverage limits, and simple policy structures that are easy for people with limited financial knowledge to understand.

Microinsurance is intended to help protect people against financial losses caused by events such as illness, crop failure, theft, or natural disasters. This type of insurance can help people in economically vulnerable communities better manage risks and protect themselves from unexpected financial hardship. This, in turn, can help to promote economic stability and development in these communities.

One solution to natural disasters that has emerged in recent years is microinsurance. This is designed to help people who earn less than US$2 a day and who live in poverty. In the event of a catastrophic event, such as the loss of income due to a natural disaster, microinsurance helps protect their assets and prevents them from falling into poverty. Another innovative solution is parametric insurance, which uses weather maps to predict and payout to people in areas hit by catastrophic events.

Parametric insurance

Parametric insurance is a type of insurance that pays out when a specific triggering event occurs, such as a natural disaster, and does not require a lengthy claims process or investigation. Instead, payment is determined based on a predetermined, objective index or parameter, such as the intensity of an earthquake or the wind speed of a hurricane, that is directly related to the event being insured against. This allows for a faster claims settlement process, as the payout is based solely on the parameter being met and not on the actual loss suffered by the insured party. Parametric insurance is often used to provide coverage for events that are difficult to predict, such as weather-related disasters, and can be especially useful for businesses and individuals in areas that are prone to such events.

Both of these solutions are examples of how technology is making insurance more accessible and affordable for people in remote areas. Insurance is often seen as a necessary evil, but these innovations are changing that perception.

IN A NUTSHELL

Insurance plays an important role in mitigating financial losses associated with unexpected events. However, it is important for individuals and organizations to understand the scope of their insurance coverage and to take steps to prepare for and mitigate the risks of uninsured losses. In conclusion, insurance is an important part of our lives, but many people do not have access to it. Microinsurance and parametric insurance are just two examples of how innovation is making insurance more accessible and affordable for people in remote areas. However, there are limits to what insurance can cover, and we need to be aware of these limitations.

DISCUSSION QUESTIONS

1   What is insurance, and why do we need it?
2   How do insurance companies work, and how do they assess risk?
3   What is reinsurance, and why do insurance companies need it?
4   What are some types of risk, and how can insurance help manage them?
5   What is microinsurance, and how does it benefit low-income individuals and communities?
6   What is parametric insurance, and how does it differ from traditional insurance?

7 How have natural disasters impacted the world in recent years, and how have insurance companies been affected by them?

8 Can insurance companies accurately predict when natural disasters will occur, and what methods do they use to do so?

9 Can you provide an example of how insurance companies respond to unprecedented events such as the COVID-19 pandemic?

10 How do insurance companies handle liabilities for catastrophic events such as oil spills?

WORKS CITED

Auronen, L. (2003). Asymmetric information: Theory and applications. *Seminar of Strategy and International Business as Helsinki University of Technology, 167*, 14–18.

Chondrogiannis, E., Andronikou, V., Karanastasis, E., Litke, A., & Varvarigou, T. (2022). Using blockchain and semantic web technologies for the implementation of smart contracts between individuals and health insurance organizations. *Blockchain: Research, 3*(2), 100049.

Keil, M., Cule, P. E., Lyytinen, K., & Schmidt, R. C. (1998). A framework for identifying software project risks. *Communications of the ACM, 41*(11), 76–83.

Patrik, G. (2006). Reinsurance. *Encyclopedia of Actuarial Science, 3*.

Semieniuk, G., Campiglio, E., Mercure, J. F., Volz, U., & Edwards, N. R. (2021). Low-carbon transition risks for finance. *Wiley Interdisciplinary Reviews: Climate Change, 12*(1), e678.

Stehr, N., & Von Storch, H. (2005). Introduction to papers on mitigation and adaptation strategies for climate change: Protecting nature from society or protecting. *Environmental Science & Policy, 8*, 537–540.

Wiklund, S. (2021). Evaluating physical climate risk for equity funds with quantitative modelling–how exposed are sustainable funds? *Journal of Sustainable Finance & Investment*, 1–26. ttps://doi.org/10.1080/20430795.2021.1894901

World Economic Forum. (2023). *10 costliest climate disasters of 2022*. Retrieved from https://www.weforum.org/agenda/2023/01/10-costliest-climate-disasters-of-2022/

CHAPTER 11

Carbon markets

WHY TO MEASURE AND REPORT CARBON EMISSIONS?

Carbon is a crucial element for all life forms on Earth. It forms complex molecules by bonding with other elements, including oxygen, hydrogen, and nitrogen. With its four valence electrons, carbon is capable of bonding with all these elements. One of the reasons why carbon is abundant on Earth is because it can bond with other elements in many different ways, creating a variety of compounds that are essential for life.

Climate change is considered a market failure due to the greenhouse gas (GHG) externality, where the cost of emissions is not borne by those conducting the activities but by future generations or people in developing countries, and carbon is an essential concept there. Economists propose policy intervention to increase the price of activities emitting GHG to provide a clear signal to guide economic decision-making and stimulate low-carbon technology innovation. Other market failures, such as a lack of information, network effects, and innovation incentives, also require policy interventions. For example, policy support may be necessary to establish networks, and subsidies for R&D can encourage the development of low-carbon technologies (Bowen, Dietz, & Hicks, 2014).

WHY DO WE NEED TO PUT A PRICE ON CARBON EMISSIONS?

Putting a price on carbon is a way to address the market failure associated with carbon emissions, which are a significant contributor to climate change. A carbon price creates a financial incentive for individuals, businesses, and governments to reduce their carbon emissions and transition to a low-carbon economy. Here are some reasons why we need to put a price on carbon, as we can see in Figure 11.1:

Helps to achieve climate goals: A carbon price can be an effective tool to help countries meet their climate goals under the Paris Agreement, which aims to limit global warming to well below 2°C above pre-industrial levels. Putting a price on carbon is a way to create a financial incentive for emissions reductions and can help to promote innovation, generate revenue, address environmental justice concerns, and achieve climate goals.

DOI: 10.4324/9781003274735-11

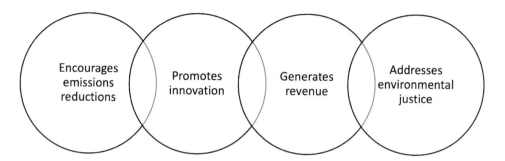

FIGURE 11.1 Some reasons to put a price on carbon emissions.

The idea that a carbon price is needed can be traced back to the work of Arthur Cecil Pigou, a University of Cambridge economist who published *The Economics of Welfare* in 1920[1] (Pigou, 2017). In this book, Pigou introduced the concept of externality and the idea that external problems could be corrected by the imposition of a charge. By externality, Pigou meant the indirect economic impact of an activity that happened outside the immediate system where the activity was occurring. The concept of externality remains central to modern welfare economics and is at the heart of environmental economics.

MECHANISMS FOR CARBON PRICING

The debate on regulatory frameworks to reduce carbon emissions generally revolves around two concepts, ETS and carbon tax:

Emissions Trading System (ETS)

An ETS, also known as cap and trade, is a market-based mechanism that some consider the most effective carbon pricing mechanism to reduce GHG emissions at the lowest possible cost to society. An ETS works on a cap-and-trade principle where regulators set a cap on total GHG emissions from covered sources, then reduce the cap over time, so emissions fall. Within the cap, covered entities generally either receive free allowances to protect installations from carbon leakage or have to buy them either through auctions or from a secondary market. Free allocations are determined by benchmarks, set at best available technology, granting the most efficient plants most of their allowances for free. Generally, covered entities must surrender at the end of the compliance period enough allowances to cover all of their emissions or face monetary penalties. Entities that reduce emissions and have extra allowances can bank them for a future compliance period (this is limited and country-specific) or sell them to another entity that is short of allowances. The trading of surplus allowances on the carbon market sets the price for emission allowances.

Main challenges of ETS

ETS is a market-based approach to controlling carbon emissions. While ETS has several potential benefits, such as reducing emissions and providing economic incentives for innovation, it also faces a number of challenges. Some of the main challenges of ETS are:

Setting the right cap: The success of ETS depends on setting an appropriate cap on emissions. If the cap is too high, it may not effectively reduce emissions. If the cap is too low, it may lead to higher carbon prices and economic disruption.

Market volatility: ETS markets can be volatile, which can make it difficult for companies to plan and invest. Carbon prices can fluctuate based on changes in supply and demand or political and regulatory factors.

Lack of international coordination: ETS is most effective when it is implemented on a global scale, but coordination among countries can be challenging. Some countries may be more reluctant to implement ETS or may have different goals and priorities.

Risk of carbon leakage: Carbon leakage occurs when companies move production to countries with lower carbon standards to avoid the costs of ETS. This can undermine the effectiveness of ETS in reducing global emissions.

Enforcement and monitoring: ETS requires strong enforcement and monitoring to prevent fraud and ensure compliance with regulations. This can be challenging, particularly in countries with weaker governance structures.

Political opposition: ETS can be politically controversial, particularly among industries that may face higher costs as a result of carbon pricing. This can make it challenging to implement or maintain ETS policies over the long term.

Overall, ETS faces several challenges, including setting the right cap, market volatility, lack of international coordination, risk of carbon leakage, enforcement and monitoring, and political opposition. To be effective, ETS policies must be carefully designed and implemented and must address these challenges effectively. Some of the main challenges for ETS are shown in Figure 11.2.

Mandatory and voluntary markets

Mandatory carbon markets are created by government regulations that require companies to purchase or trade carbon credits to meet specific emissions reduction targets. These markets are often established as part of a broader climate policy or regulatory framework, such as a cap-and-trade system or carbon tax. Companies that exceed their emissions targets can sell their excess carbon credits to other companies that are struggling to meet their targets.

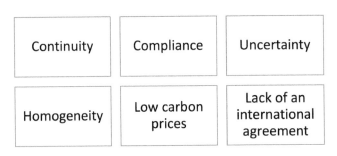

FIGURE 11.2 Some of the main challenges for ETS.

Voluntary carbon markets are created by companies or individuals who want to reduce their carbon footprint and offset their emissions voluntarily. These markets are not governed by government regulations and are not legally binding. Participants in voluntary carbon markets can purchase carbon credits from projects that generate carbon offsets, such as renewable energy projects or reforestation projects, and use them to offset their own emissions.

The key difference between mandatory and voluntary carbon markets is the regulatory framework that governs them. In both mandatory and voluntary carbon markets, the goal is to incentivize emissions reductions and encourage the development of low-carbon technologies and projects. However, mandatory carbon markets are typically larger and more established, as they are often backed by government regulations and may involve larger volumes of carbon credits and higher trading volumes. Voluntary carbon markets are often smaller and more niche but are growing rapidly as more companies and individuals seek to reduce their carbon footprint and address climate change.

CARBON MARKETS IN THE UNITED STATES

Carbon markets are an important tool for reducing GHG emissions and promoting sustainable development. While the United States has been slow to adopt national-level carbon pricing policies, several states and regions have taken steps to implement cap-and-trade systems and other carbon pricing mechanisms.

One of the most significant carbon markets in the United States is the Regional Greenhouse Gas Initiative (RGGI), which is a cap-and-trade system that involves the power sector in nine states and provinces in the United States. The RGGI was first implemented in 2009 and covers power plants with a capacity of 25 megawatts or greater. Under the RGGI, participating states set a cap on GHG emissions from the power sector and issue allowances that can be traded among participants. This system has been successful in reducing GHG emissions from the power sector while also generating revenue for participating states.

In 2015, California, the world's eighth-largest economy, introduced its own cap-and-trade system. This state-wide system covers the power sector and large industrial facilities, which account for around 85% of California's GHG emissions. The California cap-and-trade system sets a cap on emissions and allows companies to buy and sell allowances on the open market. The system has been successful in reducing GHG emissions while also generating revenue for the state.

In addition to these regional carbon markets, several other US states have implemented carbon pricing mechanisms, including carbon taxes and carbon fee-and-dividend systems. These policies have been successful in reducing GHG emissions and promoting renewable energy development. Despite these successes, the United States has yet to implement a national carbon pricing policy, which has limited the effectiveness of carbon markets and other carbon pricing mechanisms.

Carbon tax

A carbon tax is a government-set price that emitters must pay for each ton of GHG emissions they produce. This tax encourages businesses and consumers to take steps, such as using cleaner fuels or adopting new technologies, to reduce their emissions and lower their carbon tax liability. A carbon tax is usually implemented as a toll on emissions, based on the amount of produced goods or services that are typically GHG-intensive, such as a carbon tax on gasoline. This form of tax makes its implementation and collection easier on the regulator.

Compared to a cap-and-trade program, a carbon tax provides a higher level of certainty about costs but not about the level of emission reduction to be achieved. In a cap-and-trade system, the government sets a limit on the amount of GHG emissions allowed, and companies can buy and sell emission permits. This provides more certainty about emission reductions, but the costs can vary depending on the market price of permits.

THE DETERMINANTS OF CARBON PRICE DYNAMICS

Observing the prices of CO_2 and examining trading patterns within the EU ETS reveals several key insights. First, regardless of the allocation criteria being used, the initial permit endowments play a significant role in the formation of permit prices. Additionally, many installations are taking a speculative position rather than solely focusing on meeting compliance requirements by the end of each year. Finally, the strategic behavior of individual companies, rather than just the aggregated pollution volume, is a crucial factor in the price dynamics of the carbon market. These findings highlight the importance of understanding the behavior of individual actors and the initial allocation of permits in shaping the functioning of carbon markets.

DIFFERENT CORPORATE CARBON PRICING APPROACHES

There are different alternatives to determine prices for carbon, i.e., carbon fees and shadow prices.

Carbon fee

A carbon fee, also known as a carbon tax (when implemented by a regulator), is a policy tool used to incentivize a reduction in GHG emissions. It works by placing a fee on the production, distribution, or consumption of fossil fuels such as coal, oil, and gas. The fee is based on the amount of carbon dioxide or other GHG emissions produced by the fuel. The aim of a carbon fee is to make it more expensive to use fossil fuels and to encourage the use of cleaner, renewable energy sources. The fee can be levied at different points in the supply chain. The fee can be set at a fixed rate per unit of emissions or can be set to increase over time to provide a greater incentive to reduce emissions.

The revenue generated by a carbon fee can be used for various purposes, such as investing in renewable energy, funding research and development of new technologies, or providing rebates to households and businesses to offset the increased costs of energy. The effectiveness of a carbon fee depends on the level of the fee and the degree to which it encourages a shift to cleaner, low-carbon alternatives. Some argue that a carbon fee is a more efficient and cost-effective approach to reducing emissions than other policy tools, such as regulations or subsidies.

Shadow pricing

A shadow price is an estimated price used in economic analysis that reflects the true economic cost or benefit of a particular activity or resource that is not captured by market prices. It is used to estimate the value of resources or activities that do not have a market price, such as environmental resources or social costs. For example, in the context of climate change policy, a shadow price on carbon emissions could be used to estimate the true cost of emitting carbon dioxide into the atmosphere.

This shadow price would reflect the negative impacts of carbon emissions on the environment, such as the contribution to climate change, and could be used to inform policy decisions about how to reduce emissions or encourage the adoption of cleaner technologies. Shadow prices are often used in cost-benefit analysis and other economic models to evaluate the economic viability of different projects or policy options. They are typically estimated based on a combination of empirical data, scientific research, and expert opinions.

Implicit carbon price

An implicit carbon price is a value placed on carbon emissions that is not directly specified by a carbon pricing mechanism, such as a carbon tax or cap-and-trade system. It is often used as a way to measure the effectiveness of policies or regulations that indirectly affect carbon emissions, such as renewable energy mandates or energy efficiency standards. The implicit carbon price is calculated by dividing the additional cost of reducing carbon emissions by the amount of emissions reduced.

The implicit carbon price can help to assess the effectiveness and efficiency of different policies aimed at reducing carbon emissions. It can also be used to inform policy decisions about which measures are most cost-effective in achieving emission reduction targets. However, it's worth noting that the implicit carbon price is an estimate and can vary depending on the assumptions and methodologies used in the analysis. As a result, it is typically used in combination with other metrics to provide a more comprehensive picture of a country or region's carbon footprint.

Benchmarks for carbon pricing

Setting a price on carbon emissions is a complex task that involves a range of factors, including the heterogeneity of industries and geographies. Carbon pricing is a mechanism to put a cost on the GHG emissions that are causing climate change. It can be done through different approaches, such as carbon taxes or cap-and-trade systems.

However, determining the appropriate price of carbon emissions is a challenging task. Carbon prices can range from as low as US$1 to as high as US$200 per tonne of CO_2 equivalent. The price depends on a range of factors, such as the level of economic development, energy intensity, and carbon intensity of different industries and regions.

Industries vary widely in their carbon emissions, with some emitting much more than others. For example, the transportation sector contributes a significant portion of global emissions, while the agriculture sector may contribute much less. Similarly, some regions may be more carbon-intensive than others due to factors such as the use of coal for energy production, transportation systems, and industrial activity.

As a result, setting a uniform price on carbon emissions that works for all industries and regions can be challenging. A single carbon price may be too high for some industries or regions, making them uncompetitive or forcing them to shut down, while being too low for others, leading to insufficient incentives for emissions reductions.

Therefore, many countries have adopted a differentiated approach to carbon pricing, with different carbon prices for different industries and regions. For example, in the European Union, different carbon prices are set for different sectors, with higher prices for the most carbon-intensive industries. Similarly, some countries have implemented regional carbon pricing schemes to account for differences in carbon intensity between regions.

SCOPES FOR EMISSIONS

The scopes for GHG emissions refer to the categories of emissions that are included in the measurement and reporting of a company's GHG emissions. The scopes were developed by the Greenhouse Gas Protocol and are widely used as a standard framework for corporate carbon accounting. The three scopes for GHG emissions are:

Scope 1: Direct emissions from sources that are owned or controlled by the company.
Scope 2: Indirect emissions from the consumption of purchased electricity, heat, and steam that are used by the company. These emissions occur at the source of energy production, such as a power plant.
Scope 3: Indirect emissions from sources that are not owned or controlled by the company but are related to its activities, such as emissions from the production of raw materials, transportation of products, and disposal of waste. These emissions often represent the largest share of the carbon footprint and can be the most challenging to measure and manage.

It is important for organizations to consider all three scopes of GHG emissions when assessing their environmental impact and developing strategies for reducing their carbon footprint. The three different scopes for carbon emissions can also be observed in Figure 11.3.

INTERNATIONAL EFFORTS AIMING TO CURB CARBON EMISSIONS

The Kyoto Protocol

The Kyoto Protocol was an international treaty that was adopted in 1997 with the objective of reducing GHG emissions. The treaty was named after the city of Kyoto in Japan, where it was negotiated and signed. The Kyoto Protocol set binding targets for the reduction of emissions of six GHGs, including carbon dioxide, methane, and nitrous oxide.

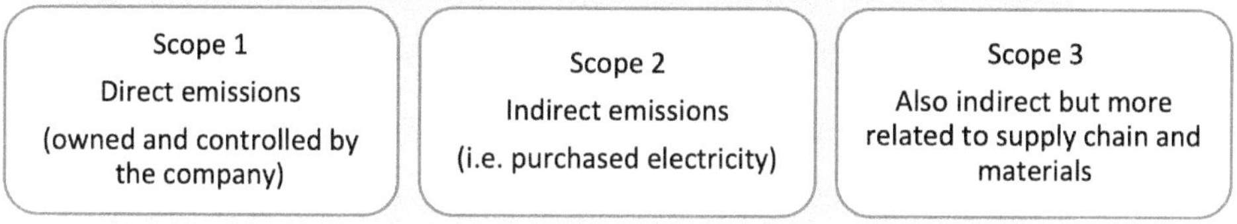

Scope 1	Scope 2	Scope 3
Direct emissions (owned and controlled by the company)	Indirect emissions (i.e. purchased electricity)	Also indirect but more related to supply chain and materials

FIGURE 11.3 Schematic representation of different scopes for carbon emissions.

Under the Kyoto Protocol, developed countries agreed to reduce their GHG emissions by an average of 5.2% below their 1990 levels by the period between 2008 and 2012. To achieve these targets, the treaty introduced three flexible mechanisms, including the Clean Development Mechanism (CDM).

The Kyoto Protocol was widely regarded as a landmark agreement in the fight against climate change, as it was the first legally binding agreement to set targets for reducing GHG emissions (Böhringer, 2003). However, the effectiveness of the treaty was limited by the fact that some of the world's largest emitters, including the United States and China, did not sign the agreement. The Kyoto Protocol expired, and was replaced by the Paris Agreement.

The Paris Agreement

The Paris Agreement (2015) is a legally binding international treaty adopted in 2015 under the United Nations Framework Convention on Climate Change (UNFCCC). It aims to limit global warming to well below 2°C above pre-industrial levels, with the goal of limiting it to 1.5°C, by reducing GHG emissions.

The Paris Agreement requires all signatory countries to set and report on their targets for reducing GHG emissions every five years, as well as to regularly report on their progress. It also calls for increased financial and technological support to developing countries to help them transition to a low-carbon economy.

The Paris Agreement is essential because it represents a global effort to address the urgent and growing threat of climate change. It recognizes that climate change is a global problem that requires collective action from all countries and all sectors of society. It also provides a framework for cooperation and collaboration among nations, businesses, and other stakeholders to accelerate the transition to a low-carbon economy.

Furthermore, the Paris Agreement is critical for the future of our planet and the well-being of current and future generations. It aims to limit the worst impacts of climate change, such as rising sea levels, extreme weather events, and loss of biodiversity, among others. By reducing

GHG emissions and transitioning to a low-carbon economy, we can ensure a sustainable future for ourselves and future generations.

Net zero

Net zero (Deutch, 2020) refers to a state where the amount of GHG emissions produced by human activities is equal to the amount removed from the atmosphere. In other words, it is a balance between emissions and the removal of GHGs.

To achieve net zero, emissions need to be reduced as much as possible through measures such as energy efficiency, renewable energy, and sustainable transportation, among others. Any remaining emissions can be offset through natural or artificial means, such as reforestation, afforestation, or carbon capture and storage.

Net zero is a critical target for mitigating climate change and limiting its impact on the planet. The Intergovernmental Panel on Climate Change (IPCC) has identified it as a necessary goal to limit global warming to 1.5°C above pre-industrial levels and avoid the worst impacts of climate change (IPCC, 2022).

Achieving net zero requires a collective effort from governments, businesses, and individuals. Governments must set targets, develop policies, and implement measures that encourage the transition to a low-carbon economy. Businesses need to invest in renewable energy, energy efficiency, and sustainable practices. Individuals can contribute by adopting more sustainable lifestyles and supporting policies and initiatives that promote a transition to a net-zero future.

WHAT IS THE DIFFERENCE BETWEEN NET ZERO AND CARBON REDUCTION?

Net zero and low carbon are related but distinct concepts. Low carbon refers to a state where GHG emissions are significantly reduced but not eliminated entirely. In contrast, net zero refers to a state where GHG emissions are balanced by the removal of an equivalent amount of emissions from the atmosphere.

In other words, achieving a low-carbon state involves reducing GHG emissions through measures such as energy efficiency, renewable energy, and sustainable transportation. However, it does not necessarily mean that emissions are eliminated entirely. A net-zero state, on the other hand, requires emissions to be reduced as much as possible, and any remaining emissions are offset through natural or artificial means, such as reforestation or carbon capture technology.

Another difference between net zero and low carbon is the level of ambition. Net zero is a more ambitious goal than low carbon because it requires not only reducing emissions but also removing any remaining emissions from the atmosphere. Achieving net zero is a crucial step in mitigating climate change and limiting its impact on the planet. While both net zero and low carbon involve reducing GHG emissions, net zero is a more ambitious target that requires not only significant emissions reductions but also a balance between emissions and removals of GHGs.

IN A NUTSHELL

Carbon markets are essential for sustainable finance (SF) as they provide a mechanism to incentivize and finance the transition toward a low-carbon economy. Carbon markets work by setting a price on carbon emissions, creating a financial incentive for companies to reduce their emissions and invest in low-carbon technologies. The revenue generated from carbon pricing can be used to finance climate-friendly projects such as renewable energy, energy efficiency, and carbon capture and storage. By channeling financial resources toward low-carbon projects, carbon markets help to support sustainable economic growth while reducing GHG emissions.

Furthermore, carbon markets provide an opportunity for companies to demonstrate their commitment to sustainability and carbon reduction. By participating in carbon markets, companies can showcase their efforts to reduce emissions and improve their environmental performance, which can enhance their reputation and attract socially responsible investors. Carbon markets are also crucial for achieving the goals of the Paris Agreement, which aims to limit global temperature rise to below 2°C above pre-industrial levels. The use of carbon markets can help countries and companies to meet their emission reduction targets in a cost-effective manner and enable them to achieve net-zero emissions by 2050.

DISCUSSION QUESTIONS

1 What are the differences between mandatory and voluntary carbon markets?
2 How do mandatory carbon markets work, and what is their regulatory framework?
3 How do voluntary carbon markets work, and what motivates companies or individuals to participate in them?
4 Why do we need to put a price on carbon, and what are some benefits of doing so?
5 What is an externality, and how is it related to the idea of carbon pricing?
6 What is an emissions trading system, and how does it work to reduce GHG emissions?
7 What are the different approaches to corporate carbon pricing, and how do they differ?
8 What are the benchmarks for carbon pricing, and how are they established?
9 What are the scopes for emissions? Give examples of what each of them includes.
10 What is the difference between the Kyoto Protocol and the Paris Agreement, and what are their goals?

NOTE

1 Although The Economics of Welfare was originally published in 1920, several versions of the book have been published since.

WORKS CITED

Böhringer, C. (2003). The Kyoto protocol: A review and perspectives. *Oxford Review of Economic Policy, 19*(3), 451–466.

Bowen, A., Dietz, S., & Hicks, N. (2014). *Why do economists describe climate change as a market failure?* Retrieved from https://www.lse.ac.uk/granthaminstitute/explainers/why-do-economists-describe-climate-change-as-a-market-failure/

Deutch, J. (2020). Is net zero carbon 2050 possible? *Joule, 4*(11), 2237–2240.

Intergovernmental Panel on Climate Change. (2022). *Climate change 2022 mitigation of climate change.* Author.

Paris Agreement. (2015, December). Paris agreement. In *Report of the conference of the parties to the United Nations Framework Convention on Climate Change* (Vol. 4, p. 2017), 21st session, Paris. HeinOnline.

Pigou, A. (2017). *The economics of welfare.* Taylor & Francis, 2017.

CHAPTER 12

Transition to clean energy

WHAT IS RENEWABLE ENERGY?

Renewable energy refers to energy sources that can be replenished as quickly as they are consumed or even faster. Examples of renewable energy technologies include biomass, wind energy, hydroelectric power, and solar photovoltaic systems. While each technology has its own advantages and drawbacks, there are numerous other options available. However, it's important to note that not all renewable energy sources are inherently clean.

Some renewable energy technologies can help us achieve both sustainability and cleanliness goals, while others may only fulfill one of these objectives. Renewable energy is sustainable and can be considered an almost inexhaustible source of energy. For instance, instead of relying on the slow decomposition of dinosaurs over thousands of years to produce petroleum, we can directly generate heat by incinerating waste materials. This approach promotes more sustainable energy production and has the potential to significantly reduce carbon emissions. Modern biomass processing methods can also facilitate efficient carbon dioxide (CO_2) sequestration while minimizing waste sent to landfills.

CAN THE WHOLE WORLD BE POWERED ON RENEWABLES?

Maybe. This is also an important thing to mention on the energy transition topic. Why? Because in the case of fossil fuels, there is actually a reason why we were so dependent on them for so many years (Armaroli & Balzani, 2011). On the one hand, reliability, but, on the other, self-containment. There is a practical reason why we like to use oil so much. We can conveniently store it in a tank and use the energy from it at will. Think about an internal combustion car as an example.

ENERGY FLOW AND STOCK

There we can observe how different technologies started to evolve for practical reasons. Think about how the wood had an early start as a power source as it was readily available and practical.

DOI: 10.4324/9781003274735-12

As technology advanced, we found out that coal was perhaps a better alternative than wood, and extraction was too off. And so petroleum and natural gas took their turn according to what technology would allow, the demand for that particular source of energy, and even political priorities or preferences.

Along came renewables, but they had their own challenges. Solar energy only works effectively when the sun is shining, and that does not assure reliability, as we also need energy at night to watch the news or our favorite show. Wind energy is only good when the wind is blowing, and that again can depend on other factors. And that would also yield intermittence, or basically energy production from renewables occurs at irregular intervals that are not continuous. In other words, we cannot use energy just anytime. Reliability is what helped build the case for fossil fuels, as you can produce energy as long as you have a match. That is why we depend so much on fossil fuels, as long as you have a box of matches because fuels are a stock of energy. Energy in fuels is self-contained.

And that takes us to another aspect that is also important for production and consumption of energy. As energy needs to flow, at least when it is not contained or stored. That is the big challenge of renewables and storage. Renewables can be a great solution to produce energy with reduced impact and even continuously as long as we can match that production with consumption, or supply and demand as we know it from economics. Perhaps we can get a better view from Figures 12.1–12.4.

As we can see here, the energy produced by the United States in this example is allocated for consumption in four main sectors: residential, commercial, industrial, and transportation. In the meanwhile, the world that we live in today has found new innovative ways to shift change, as electric cars are now a reality, and we do not need to depend anymore on petroleum as the main source of power transportation. We are already headed toward electrification

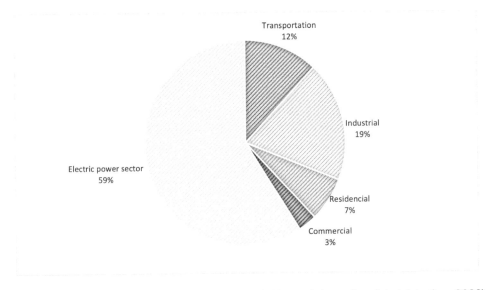

FIGURE 12.1 Renewable energy by use sector (US Energy Information Administration, 2023).

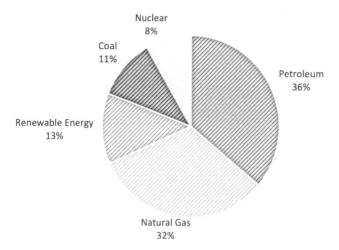

FIGURE 12.2 Energy mix in the United States, according to the source (US Energy Information Administration, 2023).

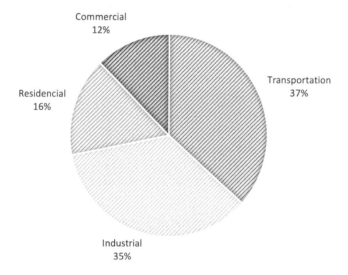

FIGURE 12.3 Energy mix in the United States, according to use (US Energy Information Administration, 2023).

for transportation, and other sources and uses are also changing now, i.e., hydrogen and other alternative fuels for industrial, commercial, and transportation.

There are several ways to provide that resiliency with renewables, and technology already exists in many cases, but it takes time to transition. Significant investments are needed, and policies need to be aligned.

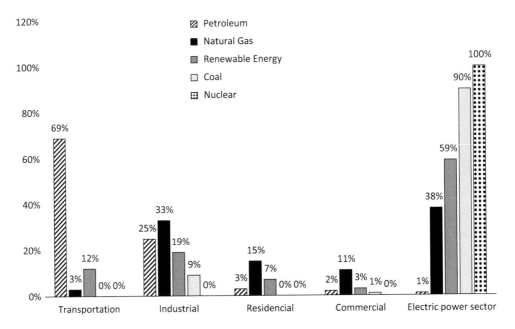

FIGURE 12.4 Distribution of energy sourced by use sector (US Energy Information Administration, 2023).

ENERGY TRANSITION

Even in the United States, our grid network and many other places in the world is kind of a patchwork system of regulated and unregulated utilities. Utilities basically bounce different energy sources to supply the energy that is in demand. Some sources are more reliable than others, while others are cleaner than others. A mix of energy will be promoted as long as the service of energy is provided, but that is only short-term thinking. An energy transition requires investment and a well-planned long-term strategy. Especially to source peak-hour production of energy.

WHY IS RENEWABLE ENERGY IMPORTANT?

Renewable energy is important for several reasons, including:

Reducing greenhouse gas emissions: Renewable energy sources such as solar, wind, and hydropower produce little to no greenhouse gas emissions. Switching to renewable energy can help to reduce the carbon footprint of our energy production and consumption and mitigate the effects of climate change.

Energy security: Using renewable energy can help to enhance energy security by diversifying the sources of energy supply and reducing reliance on finite and potentially volatile resources such as oil and gas.

Job creation: The renewable energy sector can create jobs and support local economies.

Economic benefits: Renewable energy can offer economic benefits such as reducing energy costs, improving energy efficiency, and reducing reliance on imported energy sources.

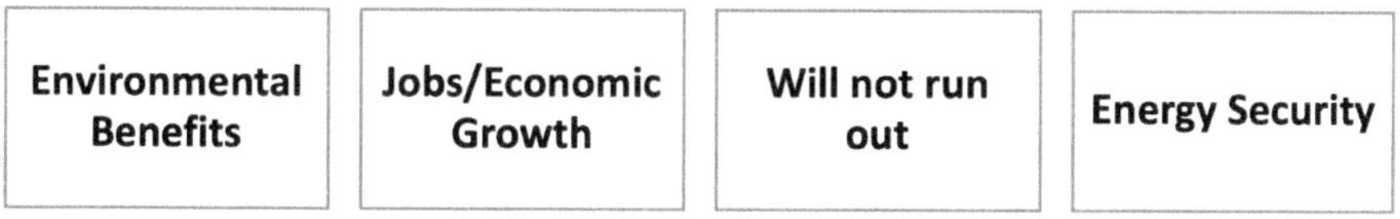

Environmental Benefits	Jobs/Economic Growth	Will not run out	Energy Security

FIGURE 12.5 Some actual benefits from renewable energy.

Environmental benefits: Renewable energy sources have lower environmental impacts than fossil fuels. For example, wind and solar energy require less land use and have lower water use than conventional energy sources.

Public health benefits: Switching to renewable energy can reduce air pollution and associated health problems, such as respiratory illnesses and premature deaths, caused by burning fossil fuels.

Renewable energy is important because it offers a range of benefits, including reducing greenhouse gas emissions, enhancing energy security, creating jobs, offering economic and environmental benefits, and improving public health. As the world continues to face the challenge of climate change, transitioning to renewable energy sources is becoming increasingly important (Dincer, 2000). It can also be observed in Figure 12.5.

SOME EXAMPLES OF RENEWABLE ENERGY TECHNOLOGIES

Renewable energy can come in different forms and natures, with specific characteristics.

Solar (Ferry & Monoian, 2012)

People love solar panels. Solar panels make a statement if you see them installed on top of a corporate office building. In short, solar panels can tell the story that the company is very forward-thinking, and it's actually sending a message that it is eco-friendly. I don't know why solar panels are so trendy and fancy, but they are. And that also applies to residential solar. If you have them at home, they look good, but they also tell the story that this household is helping the environment. However, the downside of solar is that they are not always the most profitable investment. If you live in an area that does not offer subsidies, solar Present Value can take up to seven or nine years to pay back. Although it can be faster in other areas, solar prices continue to reduce. But payback in solar is still dependent on different factors, and sometimes prices do not show reductions, as we can observe in Figure 12.6.

They also have other benefits; they are easy to finance and easy to scale. And those are huge aspects. In many places, you can find banks and other financial institutions that have already had the experience of financing solar. They know the technology, so they can understand it and therefore finance it. They know what to expect. It is a simple technology to work with. There are different technologies available, but usually better-known, well-established technologies are easier to finance. Because in the case of financing, the more the financier knows the technology, the easier it is for them to project its performance, risk, return, etc.

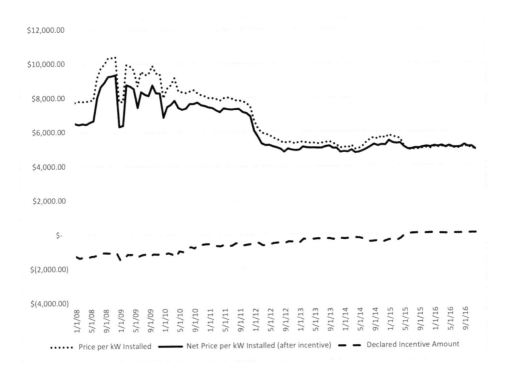

FIGURE 12.6 The historical cost of photovoltaic panel systems by kW in California, own illustration. Data in USD (Vargas & Chesney, 2021b).

Also, many companies that sell the panels offer a package deal where they basically provide financing for the equipment they sell and even install. And in some cases, this has allowed solar to become so popular in some areas.

Solar panels can be scalable like Legos. I do not mean that literally, but they can be installed and further expanded on a modular basis. So, if you start small, you can then decide to grow the project later. It's fairly easy, as you would just need to install the extra panels to increase capacity. Photovoltaic panels also have other benefits, i.e., they can produce energy for 20–25 years on average. They also require relatively little maintenance if there is no maintenance other than cleaning in some cases.

One also needs to take into account the fact that fossil fuels are heavily subsidized. The fact that now solar energy is commercially attractive is even more interesting. So even with fossil fuels as an alternative, renewables, and particularly solar, are starting to make headlines because they are becoming more accessible and cheaper at a fast pace. As prices continue to reduce, we will reach economies of scale, and solar and other technologies will gain more acceptance, and prices will continue to reduce until they reach a fair level.

Regarding the cost of energy production, please keep in mind that with renewables, we usually make an investment that would yield energy for a long time, i.e., 20–25 years, in the case of solar photovoltaic. And that is a different kind of setting that we get with fuels, as we then buy the fuel that will be combusted to produce energy. And although prices sometimes seem higher for renewable energy, we need to levelize prices to observe their actual cost. Levelized prices are prices that are adjusted to account for the required investment needed for that technology to work, basically to have an all-included cost that allows for a fairer comparison among different technologies.

Wind (Ferry & Monoian, 2012)

Wind energy is a renewable energy source that harnesses the power of wind to generate electricity. This is done through the use of wind turbines, which consist of large blades that rotate when the wind blows over them. As the blades turn, they spin a generator, which produces electricity that can be used to power homes, businesses, and communities. Wind energy is considered to be one of the cleanest and most sustainable forms of energy, as it produces no emissions or pollutants and has a relatively low impact on the environment. It is also becoming increasingly cost-effective, making it a popular choice for those looking to reduce their carbon footprint and invest in a more sustainable future. As technology advances, it is likely that wind energy will continue to play an important role in the global shift toward renewable energy.[1] Somehow, a lot of people do not really like wind energy because they do not like looking at turbines outside of their windows. Even when you have wind turbines not too far from your home, you can sometimes get a very spooky shade at certain times of the day, and that can be creepy.

Geothermal (Ferry & Monoian, 2012)

In the case of geothermal, this is one that has been popular in recent years. It is interesting because, in reality, we're just using the heat that already exists underground. The Earth is designed in such a way that we actually take advantage of it, and we actually produce heat or produce energy from geothermal.[2] Sometimes I find it a little bit boring. It sounds like something we would hear from, I don't know, like a Star Wars episode or something, or perhaps something in Iceland or somewhere really far away, and it's actually a very big thing in Iceland.

INCENTIVES SCHEMES

Incentive schemes for renewable energy vary by country and region, but here are a few examples:

Feed-in tariffs (FITs): This is a scheme where solar power producers are paid a premium rate for the electricity they generate and feed into the grid. The rate is typically higher than the retail electricity price and is set by the government or utility company. FITs are common in many countries, including Germany, Japan, and the United Kingdom.

Net metering: This is a billing arrangement where solar power producers are credited for the excess electricity they generate and feed into the grid. The credits can be used to offset the electricity they draw from the grid when their solar panels are not generating enough power, such as at night or during cloudy weather. Net metering is available in many states in the United States and in some other countries.

Tax credits: Governments offer tax credits to incentivize homeowners and businesses to install solar panels. In the United States, for example, homeowners can claim a federal tax credit of up to 26% of the cost of their solar panel system.

Rebates: Some governments offer rebates to homeowners and businesses that install solar panels. The rebate amount varies by region and can be a percentage of the system cost or a fixed amount.

Green certificates: Also known as Renewable Energy Certificates (RECs), these are trad-able certificates that represent the environmental attributes of the electricity generated from renewable sources, such as solar. RECs are issued by governments or third-party organizations and can be sold to companies or individuals who want to offset their carbon footprint or meet renewable energy targets.

These are just a few examples of the many incentive schemes available for renewable energy. The specific schemes available will depend on your location and the policies of your government and utility companies.

LICENSE TO OPERATE

The other aspect that we do not hear about so frequently is nuclear waste. No one wants to take care of the residues that result from nuclear production, and that is not an isolated event. That is day-to-day for those countries where nuclear energy is deployed. What do we do with nuclear waste? Of course, not in my backyard, but please source my energy when I need it. What I mean is that we are using energy, but we do not want to be respon-sible for the waste that will be produced. There are solutions that have been proposed in that regard, and perhaps as the Germans think, for example, that nuclear waste should be kept safely in a place that can be easily reached so that it can be recycled once we have the technology necessary to do it properly. To me, it makes sense, and perhaps it is reasonable to consider. Others think that we should send it to space and never think about it, and it could also be a solution, but, nevertheless, we are producing nuclear waste, and we do not want to deal with the effects. And nuclear waste is a risky matter. It is something we can be certain about.

VIABILITY

Implementing a renewable energy power project requires careful planning and execution. The following requirements must be met to ensure a successful implementation, as can be seen in Figure 12.7.

1   *Experienced development team*: An experienced development team is necessary to ensure that the project is designed, planned, and executed properly. The team should include profes-sionals such as engineers, project managers, and financial analysts.
2   *Sizable projects*: To make the project viable and cost-effective, it must be of a sizable scale. The project should generate enough electricity to be sold to the grid or to a customer. A larger project may also have more funding and revenue-generating potential.

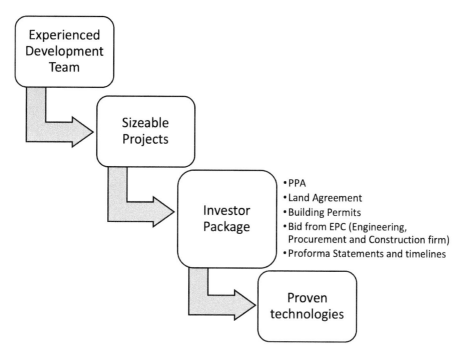

FIGURE 12.7 Basic requirements for a successful implementation of a renewable energy project.

3 *Investor package*: An investor package should be created to attract investors and secure funding. This package should include financial projections, risk assessments, and a detailed project plan. This should include the following as well:

    a *Power Purchase Agreement (PPA)*: A PPA is a contract between the power generator and the electricity buyer. It establishes the terms and conditions for the sale of electricity and can help secure funding for the project.

    b *Land Agreement*: A land agreement must be secured for the solar power project. This includes obtaining necessary permits and ensuring that the land is suitable for the project.

    c *Building Permits*: Building permits must be obtained from the local government to ensure that the solar power project is constructed in accordance with local regulations and building codes.

    d *Bid from EPC (Engineering, Procurement, and Construction Firm)*: An EPC firm is responsible for the design, procurement, and construction of the solar power project. A competitive bidding process should be conducted to select the best EPC firm for the project.

    e *Proforma Statements and Timelines*: Proforma statements and timelines must be prepared to establish the financial and operational objectives for the project. The timelines should include important milestones, such as the start and end of construction and the beginning of commercial operations.

4 *Proven technologies*: The project should use proven technologies to ensure that it is reliable and efficient. The technology used should also be scalable and easily maintained.

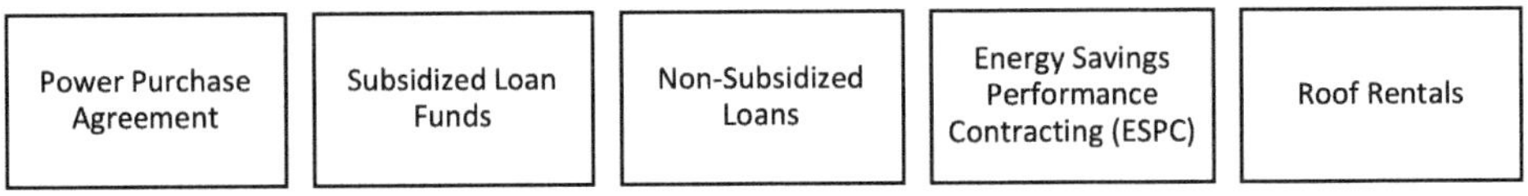

Power Purchase Agreement	Subsidized Loan Funds	Non-Subsidized Loans	Energy Savings Performance Contracting (ESPC)	Roof Rentals

FIGURE 12.8 Different financing alternatives for renewable energy.

FINANCING

Projects can be financed through a range of methods, including PPAs, subsidized and non-subsidized loans, roof rentals, etc. The financing option chosen will depend on the specific needs of the project and the financial situation of the project owner. It is important to carefully evaluate each financing option to determine the best fit for the project, as seen in Figure 12.8:

1   *PPA*: Explained above.
2   *Subsidized loan funds*: Governments and financial institutions offer subsidized loans for renewable energy projects, including solar. These loans have lower interest rates and more favorable repayment terms than standard loans, making them an attractive option for solar project financing.
3   *Regular loans*: Regular loans are another option for financing solar projects. These loans usually have higher interest rates and less favorable repayment terms than subsidized loans, but they can be easier to obtain.
4   *Energy savings performance contracting (ESPC)*: ESPC is a financing method that allows the energy savings from a project to be used to repay the cost of the project. The energy savings are guaranteed and are used to cover the cost of the project, making it a low-risk option for financing.
5   *Roof rentals*: Rooftop solar installations can be financed through roof rental agreements. Under this arrangement, a third party finances the solar project and installs the panels on the rooftop of a building. The building owner then rents the rooftop space to a third party, who sells the electricity generated by the solar panels to the grid or to the building owner.

NEXT CHALLENGES

Many challenges lie ahead for energy, but the ones that are more related to the clean energy transition are essentially two, storage and recycling.

Storage

Energy storage has a key role to play in the transition toward a carbon-neutral economy. By balancing power grids and saving surplus energy, energy storage represents a concrete means of improving energy efficiency and integrating more renewable energy sources into electricity systems (European Comission, 2023). Some storage alternatives can be seen in Figure 12.9.

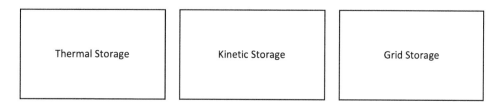

FIGURE 12.9 Some forms of storage of energy alternatives.

The next thing to make renewable energy work is storage, and it is super important as energy, and particularly electricity, needs to be used as it is produced. And storage is challenging, well, because it is costly. Perhaps subsidies are no longer needed to incentivize investment in renewable energy, but some incentives are still needed to promote storage capacity. In particular, it is relevant to create storage capacity for solar as it already works and because the market is still willing to invest in it no matter what the cost. Subsidies are needed as new technology matures, and that is the case for energy storage. This will help make it commercially feasible and can also promote the development of alternative technologies for the same purpose.

There are different ways to store energy, i.e., physical storage, which basically consists of pumping water uphill when energy is cheap or at least readily available and storing it there so it can be contained for a while. Once energy is needed, water is allowed to flow so that turbines can be activated to produce energy as water flows through them. This is a great solution and seems to work in some areas where geography allows it.

But another creative way can also be implemented, i.e., the use of mini-turbines (aka pico turbines) that can be installed in a building plumbing to generate energy as water flows in and out of the facility. We can also store energy as heat or thermal storage. For example, in those areas where geothermal is actually viable, i.e., by using an empty well or tank to store hot water to use the heat later. And then we have kinetic storage. If you remember those cars that some kids play with that you pull back, so they gain an impulse to go forward. Kinetic energy is stored as you push back the car, and it is released once the car is freed to go forward. Finally, we have grid storage. Keeping in mind that at the time I am writing this book, the grid in the United States requires a lot of investment. But if we had the conditions for this, we could just produce energy in a distributed way so that the excess energy I produce can be used by a neighbor, and their excess energy can also be used by their neighbors to create a network of distributed production. It would allow more people to produce energy locally.

Recycling

By 2030, the cumulative value of recoverable raw materials from end-of-life panels globally will be about US$450 million, which is equivalent to the cost of raw materials currently needed to produce about 60 million new panels (EPA, 2022; International Renewable Energy Agency, 2016). To put this in context, the estimated volume of scrap material for solar panels installed between 1999 and 2017 is estimated to reach almost 2 million tons, in the next two decades, solely for the United States. This means that a large amount of material has been used in the production of solar panels during this time period, but this number continues to grow as

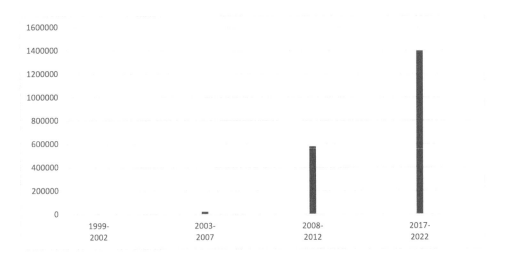

FIGURE 12.10 Amount of scrap material estimated to be produced by photovoltaic panel decommissioning in the United States, according to when panels were originally installed (in tons) (Vargas & Chesney, 2021a).

the popularity of panels also continues. To show this, the number of panels installed between 2013 and 2017 alone represented 70% of that total volume. This suggests that the use of solar panels has become more mainstream and widespread in recent years. The estimated amount of scrap material to be produced from solar panels in the United States can be observed in Figure 12.10.

However, if we estimate steady growth in the popularity of solar panels from 2018 going forward, with the same rate of average growth for the last five years, an equivalent amount of new scrap material could have been produced as early as 2020. This indicates that the use of solar panels is likely to continue to increase as more people become aware of the benefits of renewable energy and the need to reduce carbon emissions, but it still poses an important challenge for the end-of-life management of the panels.

The increasing popularity of solar panels also brings with it a need for responsible waste management and recycling of the materials used in their production. While solar panels are a sustainable energy source, their production and disposal can have negative environmental impacts if not managed properly. Therefore, it is crucial for the industry to focus on developing sustainable practices for the production and disposal of solar panels, to ensure that they remain a sustainable energy solution in the long term.

The ugly duckling, nuclear energy

Perhaps the alternative we have not discussed yet is nuclear energy. Nuclear energy is nonrenewable because it uses uranium, which is a finite resource that cannot be replenished if exhausted. However, the main controversy regarding nuclear comes from risk. As we know, there are different examples of accidents and other complications that have affected nuclear advance. Many countries have pushed back from nuclear as it has become less popular in recent times.

I do not particularly support nuclear, but for the purpose of our overview, we need to acknowledge its benefits. Nuclear has very interesting potential because of its scale and the fact that it can produce energy independently of environmental conditions. It is extremely efficient and does provide a clear solution for different areas. In fact, interesting evolvements in nuclear energy research are still under way, and we can expect to see new technologies evolve around it, i.e., fusion.

And I do not want to get political, but please consider the situation when most of the world started to depend on natural gas to source energy, as it was reliable and generally cheap, but at some point, the geopolitical environment in the world changed to complicate sourcing for an important area of Europe and Asia.

The main concern with nuclear today is safety. As new technologies evolve, perhaps some countries could reconsider their policy around it. The risk that we have with nuclear is that having one accident, one single accident, may have effects for thousands of years, and that is just ridiculous. But the actual examples that we find are the result of technologies decades old when that happened. We can certainly do better, but whether or not it will be viable is yet to be discussed.

I recently found out about Transatomic[2] (Betzler et al., 2017). This company found a way to massively extend the life of uranium and reduce the risk of nuclear plants. This allowed them to make nuclear plants safer. But they could not get to go to market. This company never got off the ground with government approvals, so it had to close the shop. But they made all the research in nuclear power open source. They had hundreds of millions from venture capitalists.

IN A NUTSHELL

Transitioning to clean, renewable energy is a vital step toward a sustainable and healthy future for both our planet and ourselves. By reducing our reliance on fossil fuels and other nonrenewable sources of energy, we can significantly reduce greenhouse gas emissions, combat climate change, and create a cleaner and healthier environment. While there are certainly challenges to making this transition, such as the need for significant investments in infrastructure and technology, the benefits far outweigh the costs. Renewable energy technologies are becoming more efficient and cost-effective, making them increasingly competitive with traditional fossil fuels.

Transitioning to clean energy presents significant environmental and economic opportunities, with the potential to create new jobs and industries and drive innovation and growth in the energy sector. Finally, the transition to clean renewable energy is a necessary step for addressing climate change. But it is also an opportunity to build a more sustainable, equitable, and prosperous future for all.

DISCUSSION QUESTIONS

1 What is renewable energy?
2 Why is renewable energy important, and what are some of its benefits?

3 Are there other sustainable technologies besides the four most important (wind, solar, hydro, and biomass) used for renewable energy?

4 What is clean energy, and what technologies can help us reach both clean and renewable energy goals?

5 Can the whole world be powered on renewable energy sources?

6 What are the challenges faced by renewable energy sources in terms of reliability and intermittence?

7 How do the production and consumption of energy relate to renewable energy?

8 What role does energy storage play in the transition toward a carbon-neutral economy, and why is it important?

9 What are some alternatives to traditional battery storage for energy?

10 What are some of the benefits and drawbacks of nuclear energy, and what are some potential solutions to nuclear waste?

NOTES

1 For further information, see the complete report: https://landartgenerator.org/LAGI-FieldGuideRenewableEnergy-ed2.pdf

2 For further reference, see http://www.transatomicpower.com/

WORKS CITED

Armaroli, N., & Balzani, V. (2011). Towards an electricity-powered world. *Energy & Environmental Science, 4*(9), 3193–3222.

Betzler, B. R., Powers, J. J., Worrall, A., Robertson, S., Dewan, L., & Massie, M. (2017). *Two-dimensional neutronic and fuel cycle analysis of the transatomic power molten salt reactor* (No. ORNL/TM-2016/742). Oak Ridge National Lab. (ORNL).

Dincer, I. (2000). Renewable energy and sustainable development: A crucial review. *Renewable and Sustainable Energy Reviews, 4*(2), 157–175.

EPA. (2022). *Solar panel recycling*. Retrieved from https://www.epa.gov/hw/solar-panel-recycling

European Comission. (2023). *Energy storage*. Retrieved March 2023, from https://energy.ec.europa.eu/topics/research-and-technology/energy-storage_en

Ferry, R., & Monoian, E. (2012). *A field guide to renewable energy technologies*. Land Art Generator Initiative.

International Renewable Energy Agency. (2016). *End-of-life management. Solar photovoltaic panels*. International Renewable Energy Agency. Retrieved from https://www.irena.org/-/media/Files/IRENA/Agency/Publication/2016/IRENA_IEAPVPS_End-of-Life_Solar_PV_Panels_2016.pdf

U.S. Energy Information Administration. (2023). *Today in energy*. Retrieved from https://www.eia.gov/

Vargas, C., & Chesney, M. (2021a). End of life decommissioning and recycling of solar panels in the United States. A real options analysis. *Journal of Sustainable Finance & Investment, 11*(1), 82–102.

Vargas, C., & Chesney, M. (2021b). What are you waiting to invest in grid-connected residential photovoltaics in California? A real options analysis. *Journal of Sustainable Finance & Investment, 13*(1), 660–677.

CHAPTER 13

Innovation, a path to follow

THE EVOLUTION OF SUSTAINABLE FINANCE

Let us start with academia. Usually, the general understanding of the evolution of sustainable finance (SF) comes from the concept of an evolution of SF, perhaps even as described by Shoenmaker, "SF 1.0 to SF 3.0" (Schoenmaker, 2018), and later by Bush and others in 2021 (Busch et al., 2021). There is an ongoing evolution, but what does this mean? SF 1.0 is how it started. It means keeping it simple. For example, to exclude investments and avoid stocks on blacklists. We are just aligning investment portfolios to individual values. And that is what evolved to become metrics for SF. In previous chapters, we discussed different applications, i.e., how ESG (environmental, social, and governance) metrics looked like the kind of metrics that financial analysts typically use.

In the case of ESG factors, the fact that you can see a particular digit, four or five, or even three, should be easy enough to interpret. Depending on the scale, higher should be better or vice versa. But it really cannot be oversimplified like that. As we also mentioned, it does not go beyond and tell you something descriptive. On one side, we have the ESG metric; on the other, we might find a more comprehensive report of over a 100 pages that get the detail. The actual metric is just data readily incorporated into the more traditional analysis. It's not the perfect metric, but it is easy to manage and interpret (in general terms). It is a good solution, but just good enough to serve its essential purpose. At this stage, we want to incorporate SF into what is already established.

SF 2.0 will then be the next stage. As we understand how sustainability creates value for Finance, we must know how to make that value. This would imply that we understand the implication of long-term value creation. Exciting work can be found by different authors on this specific idea, but one that stands out is done by Edmans, Fang, and Huang (2022). At this stage, we are also open to environmental risk as real financial risk. We attempt to understand the actual cost of decisions and activities, and by that, we also try to internalize the cost of externalities. And so, it is when we start to see more attempts to regulate SF. It is, in many ways, the stage at which most of us were experiencing the world at the time this book was written.

The next stage is SF 3.0. This progression considers an evolution that allows SF to become more comprehensive without excluding assets or forcing additional metrics into an established setting. This perhaps can be more straightforward as it contributes to value creation and risk

DOI: 10.4324/9781003274735-13

management. It contributes to creating more innovative solutions to finance that is essentially sustainable. And this means that the actual implementation at this stage considers sustainability more inherently in the process and not just as a patch that tries to cover the minimum requirements.

Beyond that, we must also consider that although stricter metrics can be developed, they would still have to fit most companies to be relevant. This means that if we made metrics that were too stringent, i.e., considered every single environmental aspect, perhaps we could not make a fit for existing companies, i.e., Apple or Google. And so, they never are good metrics, as they are two examples of companies that many investors would like to assess. There will always be trade-offs between efficacy and scope, yet we must aim to comprehensively design metrics that consider ESG and other criteria. We must find an appropriate trade-off level, remember that the critical word is correct, and attempt to maintain a proper balance. It cannot be so strict that it excludes relevant assets. It cannot be so detailed that it's impossible to report. But at the same time, it cannot be so simple that it does not say anything relevant. And that is how we get to the evolution of what we call SF 3.0 and beyond.

VALUE FOR STAKEHOLDERS

The other key driver to highlight here is stakeholder integration and value creation. As it is now, it is as simple as ticking the boxes sometimes. Still, if we go back, even the actual possibility of having those boxes, to begin with, was a huge advance from where we were coming from, and that is part of the value creation of SF. We also need to acknowledge the relevance of the role of different stakeholders, as seen in Figure 13.1, in value creation, and currently the financial system understands it. And that may also comprise the part of governments and regulators that are crucial to this process and perhaps deserve a particular category.

In Figure 13.1, we notice how diverse stakeholders can be. And so are their needs, which can be very diverse. But they all have in common a great potential to do their part. Their role in more responsible investments and consumption. And there, again, is how we can create value. It is crucial to notice how stakeholders do not refer to shareholders only, who were the central focus of traditional finance in the past.

An interesting concept of value creation for all stakeholders comes from the book *Grow the Pie* (Edmans, 2021). In sustainability, we typically aim to be more efficient and do things better, but what if we made it better for everyone? If you allow me the analogy, what if we did something to grow the pie? SF should not limit to the symbolic distribution of the pieces of the pie. We can also start thinking outside the box. Sustainability relies on efficiency because the more efficient we are, the more sustainable we become. And we see that in economics, i.e., as the return is benefit minus cost, and in Finance, i.e., profit equals income minus cost. So, the more value we generate, the more we have for everyone, but we must mind the cost. The problem is, again, how to do it? But as we figure that out, what if we make our processes more environmentally friendly and efficient? What if we reduce our waste disposal and make our water usage more clean and efficient? Those things are also inside the cost and help us create more value. And we have seen this in the different applications for SF already.

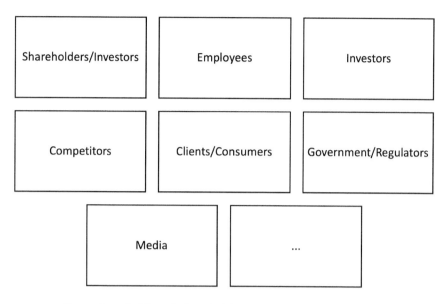

FIGURE 13.1 Examples of different shareholders.

But it is complex, and we must also put it in context to better understand it. We live in a global society, and as we try to figure out how to make more sustainable choices, we also need to keep in mind all implications that decision-making has. We are on the right track for some metrics; we just have too many metrics to mind and do not even know where to begin in some cases. Suppose we think about poverty, at least extreme poverty. We have seen fundamental advances since we came up with the idea to tackle it with the millennium goals (from 2000 to 2015),[1] the predecessors of the sustainable development goals (SDGs)[2] (from 2015 to 2030) (Sachs, 2012). Significant progress has materialized; we are just not done yet. We still need to do many things, but we can figure out innovative ways to achieve them.

Global risks are ranked severity according to the WEF (World Economic Forum, n.d.) as we recall from Figure 4.3; we can now see those same risks in a different order and observe in Table 13.1 how most of them are environmental, and the other part can somehow be aligned to social. To be fair, the WEF defines five different risk categories: Economic, Environmental, Geopolitical, Societal (social for our assessment), and Technological. And those are still reflected in the last column of Table 13.1. Still, we can also observe that none of the described risks identified for the short and long term are fundamentally economic. The single technological and geopolitical risks identified can also be grouped as social or societal risks.

THE ONLY CONSTANT IS THE CHANGE

The tsunami that was COVID-19 since 2020, the resulting pandemic in the two years that followed, and the economic debacle that resulted from it had the worst timing possible (Iqbal et al., 2021). But it did help us understand what was necessary. What our priorities should be,

TABLE 13.1 Global risks according to the WEF rearranged (World Economic Forum, n.d.)

Described Risk	Short-Term Rank	Long-Term Rank	Risk Category
Failure to mitigate climate change	4	1	Environmental
Failure of climate change adaption	7	2	Environmental
Natural disasters and extreme weather events	2	3	Environmental
Biodiversity loss and ecosystem collapse	N/A	4	Environmental
Natural resource crises	9	6	Environmental
Large-scale environmental damage incidents	6	10	Environmental
Large-scale involuntary migration	10	5	Social
Erosion of social cohesion and societal polarization	5	7	Social
Cost-of-living crisis	1	N/A	Social
Geoeconomic confrontation	3	9	Social (geopolitical)
Widespread cybercrime and cyber insecurity	8		Social (technological)

and what mattered. We had to pause for a moment and reevaluate what we regarded as necessary, and once we did that, we could reassess our new normal. That is why SF has gained so much traction since 2020. We opened up to the possibility of doing things differently. More investors were attracted to this new way of doing Finance. And as we had to start again, it became the perfect solution.

The positive part of the COVID-19 pandemic is that we significantly advanced in SF in just a couple of years, which is excellent news as we needed disruption to catalyze change. That is something that can be regarded as a positive innovation. Limitations that pushed us to find alternatives. We had to figure out ways to do the same things we would seamlessly do before the pandemic by taking advantage of technology and making more efficient use of what we had. Some positive results of the pandemic. We reduced a lot of carbon emissions and waste for a while. In some cases, we were also able to reduce energy use. And all of these are great examples that show that a more efficient, more sustainable way of living is possible.

We were convincing people that climate change is accurate and that drastic actions must be taken as a challenging task. But perhaps after what we experienced with COVID-19, more people recognized that the world is changing. In any case, we still must keep our eyes on the ball, i.e., we cannot miss the tremendous problem that single-use face mask usage created. As the main priority shifted to hygiene for apparent reasons, we need to remember its effects as well. We have a new issue and need to find new solutions there. That new trend we created is for our health, but the long-term problem created by waste must be dealt with as well.

As we advance in areas like remote work, not all carbon footprints are improving; we are just shifting them. The carbon footprint from businesses is being redistributed to homes and local communities. Outside of cities in some cases. In many parts of the world, many people are relocating to smaller cities and sometimes even non-urban areas as the potential to do remote work expands. This is, in many cases, something positive, but it also has an impact and needs to be dealt with.

Being so eager to consume again and get those things they could not get at a certain point was eventually an essential driver of delayed consumption. In some cases, it is even regarded as a temporary trend, but finally, getting backlash from people getting tired of the new dynamic can also backfire. Very sadly, we also became more reliant on e-commerce. And that resulted in packaging and, eventually, more waste. We did not solve the problem; we just learned to solve our issues Perhaps the period of recovery that followed the COVID19 pandemic, as described above, can be a good example of Jevon's paradox.

Jevon's paradox

The Jevon's paradox or Jevon's effect occurs when technological advances and sometimes regulation reduce consumption for practical reasons. However, as the new standard is set, reduction is sometimes compensated by additional consumption resulting from other demand or reductions of consumption cost from the latest technology. For example, think of a new energy-efficient vehicle that uses alternative energy. As the new technology can be more efficient, a user of this new technology might not be so mindful of using the vehicle as it costs them less. And if regulators also intervene and make more strict regulations regarding emissions for vehicles, demand for these alternative vehicles will also increase significantly. There could also be other factors affecting the overall usage of these resources. Still, ultimately, those factors will push more use or consumption so that the intended initial savings or reductions of the new technology are expected to be surpassed by the latest standards in the end, and therefore it is a paradox, as seen on Figure 13.2.

As technology advances, fewer resources are needed to produce the same effect, i.e., for a hypothetical car, the miles per gallon (MPG) of the MPG for a regular vehicle can be 20, as the hybrid version of the same vehicle could be 40 MPG, but this in no way should justify the overuse of the car just because it is more efficient.

One interesting phenomenon we also observed during the pandemic was a decrease in the use of public transportation. Many people avoided transportation significantly during the pandemic, but right after, many users avoided public transportation whenever possible to prevent infection. Uncertainty was so prevalent that there was no easy answer. Now we see efforts like the one from the government of Germany wanting to incentivize the use of public transportation with a subsidy of close to 90% of the value. Perhaps to aid the achievement of their carbon reduction ambitions or mitigate the effects of rising energy prices, but at what cost?[3]

INNOVATION IN FINANCE

Have you ever considered how money has changed over time? For thousands of years, we used to carry cash in small bags with coins or precious metals. The goal is the ultimate value reserve, and when things become complicated in modern economies, that is the go-to commodity to invest in for many. And then some guys came up with the idea that you could have money in the form of bills as the issuer's name was to be kept as an assurance of payment. For many years

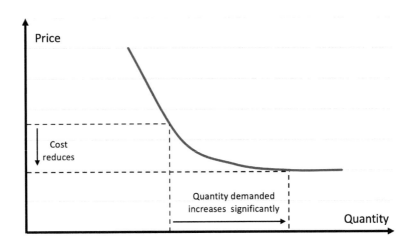

FIGURE 13.2 Example of Jevon's paradox.

it even meant that the issuer as such would have some good assets to back up their emissions until the 1970s when the US Congress decided to institute a fiat currency.[4] Still, we will not get into the rationale or soundness of the action; we will just keep it as fact for now.

Around the same time, people started to use plastic cards that once again evolved from the old concept of credit, allowing them to have purchasing power at their fingertips. Now without the burden of carrying bills and coins. For credit cards to work, a system was developed on paper with books that reported the cards that were not to be trusted, and later by electronic systems that allowed expedited validation. It was very rudimentary initially, but the much-needed evolvement set the ground for the global payment system we have today. We agreed that the critical part was that making payments was not about the money or physical currency but payment capacity.

Nowadays, we do not even need those plastics anymore. We make payments electronically, often using multipurpose devices such as smartphones or tablets. The next step, as we know, is point-to-point payments, now without intermediaries. This is the evolution of blockchain and cryptocurrencies that promise to reduce transaction costs to a minimum by reducing all middle people, without any paper trail or anything physical to back it up. It offers exciting opportunities but challenges, and it is something interesting to review in further detail at a different time.

EVERYTHING CHANGES

And the only constant today is change. It is impossible to circle ads in the newspaper if you are looking for a job. I don't think anybody has had to look for a job in the newspaper in the last ten years, at least. So basically, everything works online. These job boards and LinkedIn. And many people, if not most people today, look for jobs through these platforms. The same is true for media and streaming (Naveed, Watanabe, & Neittaanmäki, 2017), where you find platforms such as YouTube, Netflix, HBO, Prime, and many others with streaming services allowing users to find content on demand. Can you remember Blockbuster? Many years ago, families would rent movies, physical movies on VHS or later in DVD at an actual video renting location. It was not completely practical, but it was an experience. Even Netflix started by renting physical DVDs online that you would return by post. It was more practical, but the actual value was the movie, not the physical DVD, and that is why the industry migrated to streaming when technology allowed for it. And we could list hundreds or even thousands of other examples.

FINTECH

Fintech stands for financial technologies (Leong & Sung, 2018), which means the technology that provides financial services. And why is this an exciting evolution? Because for decades, big banks had patent on financial services as they controlled the money. And money was the actual currency of the financial system. Some of these big financial institutions were interested in innovation, but others were not, at least not at full speed. And so, the development of exciting innovations in the financial system came from different, sometimes unexpected sources. The more relevant examples in fintech come from money transfer and payment services. However, it is also possible to see exciting applications in lending and other traditional areas of Finance. Fintech took advantage of some inefficiencies in the financial system and found opportunities there.

In many cases, how Finance was done and regulations allowed some of these companies to thrive. Markets and users changed, and their expectations and preferences altered to allow for innovative solutions to be developed. One strength of the financial systems was relying on their presence in physical locations and branches, and even that changed rapidly over the last decade with transactions going digital. Still, some institutions must provide points of service, i.e., ATMs, but fintech institutions have found a way around this through partnerships. You still need ATMs, but not different brands, just as much as you have enough to service clients. Just enough to provide good enough service at a fair cost.

If we think about it, the purpose of ATMs is to deliver relatively small amounts of cash to clients at will in a convenient way and location. Convenience stores offer that convenient way and place and usually have excess cash at their cashiers, it is a win-win situation when they partner with fintech, and it can even potentialize the sales of the store. Some fintech companies have even partnered with convenience stores in different countries. Of course, by charging a fee, there is no free lunch. And nowadays, we can also do financial transactions with a smartphone, so no card is even needed.

Smart devices, including smartphones, tablets, laptops, etc., are the gateway to various products and services. Many consumers expect to do everything on them, which has been a game changer for different industries, including Finance. Provided that consumers drive the demand for those services, solutions need to be developed, and in most cases, they come from either the IT industries or other disruptive overlapping industries. Lots of funding is available for these implementations as the market potential is there. We also observe very much interest and support from governments and regulators to allow for some of these solutions to be implemented. Those who understand it will join the trend and evolve, while those who miss it may not take advantage of it.

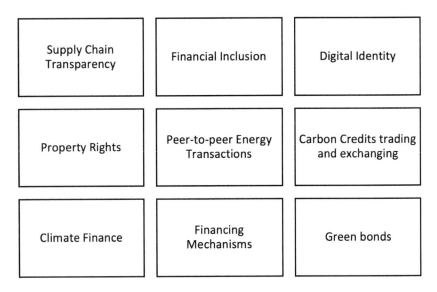

FIGURE 13.3 Fintech and SF use cases.

Fintech promotes a very interesting opportunity to solve the inefficacies of the financial system. Fintech already has an interesting opportunity as well for what they know, data management. We can see significant potential as well for implementations in every topic of SF. It makes sense, as it is technology and it involves efficiency. Some examples of uses for fintech in SF can be found in Figure 13.3.

Mpesa[5]

An interesting implementation of innovation in Finance that promotes social inclusion is MPESA in Kenya (Gikunda, Abura, & Njeru, 2014). As it was implemented some years ago, MPESA was an ideal solution as maybe it was their only alternative. Financial solutions are usually replicated in many places in the world, as they are proven to work. In the case of Kenya, we had to even start from the very beginning as there was no infrastructure for a financial system, and as a result, not many people had access to even basic financial services as they did not exist. The challenge was tremendous, and it was a time when mobile phones were not smart yet.

Let's start there. How to increase financial inclusion in Kenya? The problem was identified, and a bunch of people started to discuss how to tackle it. We are talking here about a couple of communication conglomerates, development banks, some microfinance institutions, and others. A system was implemented around 2006, and it was basically designed as a payment system. It was, of course, a very risky endeavor, as the potential outcomes were enormous, but the expected results were completely uncertain. People started to use it, and it grew to the point that it was not only used to disburse microfinance payments but it also served as a person-to-person transfer system. Of course, regulation was also an issue that had to be dealt with, particularly by proving its value, notwithstanding the need for other factors such as the technical base needed to provide reliability, safety, integrity, etc. Safaricom, the partner company for MPESA, understood that the fee revenue stream required to support this effort was not in the scope of traditional financial institutions and took the challenge of implementing it.[6]

Fast-forward many years, MPESA is still running with a very successful user base of over 30 million in Kenya and over 50 million regionally.[7] It is now used not only for payments and person-to-person transfers but even to pay salaries to employees and other very interesting applications. This is, of course, much more prosperous than the initial user base of 350,000 that they originally had in mind, and it continues to grow. This is a great example of effectively increasing financial inclusion with limited resources.

THE LIGHTBULB PARADOX

An interesting way to explain how evolution happens over time is something that we can call the lightbulb paradox (Allcott & Taubinsky, 2013). The lightbulb paradox is also represented in Figure 13.4. The environmental problems that we have today are, for certain, at least in part, the result of our decision-making of the past. And perhaps had we known better other decisions would have been made, but we did not know better, and the actual possibility is completely hypothetical as we experience those effects as a continuum, so what is the paradox of the lightbulb? Let's start with the idea that humans had to live their lives mostly during daytime for centuries, mainly because it was practical to be able to see what we were doing, and light was an essential part of it. At some point, we invented candles, and other similar devices, that, withstanding some complications, i.e., fire risk, were game changers, allowing us to enjoy the late hours of the night for different activities. When the incandescent lightbulb was invented circa the 19th century, it was a huge advance for humanity. It allowed the industry to advance as workers could be more efficient working longer hours, but also families could have more social interaction at night. It was a significant improvement from the times when candles were

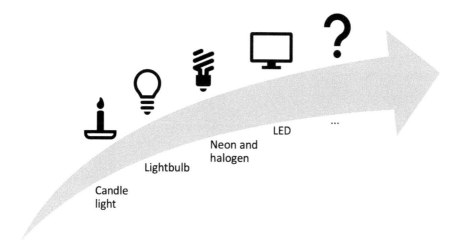

FIGURE 13.4 The lightbulb paradox.

the only alternative. It was a matter of convenience, but they also produced heat as much as light, and their consumption was high and not precisely efficient, provided that mentioned heat loss. Well, some decades passed, and of course, human ingenuity found better alternatives, and the lightbulb was not chic anymore. Halogen and neon were offering more interesting value, and they started to raise interest. They were slightly more efficient than the incandescent lightbulb, and they looked better, or at least different, and they became more desirable as a sign of the times and modernity. Until they were not, and it was not only because halogen lamps have vaporized mercury inside that can be extremely toxic if inhaled but also because we found something even better. And today, we like LEDs as the technology of choice for lighting in most use cases, and we believe that's the next best thing. Because it is more energy-efficient, it only uses a fraction of the energy required for previous technologies. It produces much less heat, and it just looks nice for our modern taste. Well, that will be the case until something new comes to the market, and that will not take even too much time. Technology continues to advance and will find even better solutions in the future.

A similar situation happens with innovation and what we understand today as SF. We do the best we can with the information and resources that we have today, but it does not mean that we will not be doing better in the future. Innovation is a continuum, and we have to keep up with it. We just have to aim to do it the best we can today.

THE ROAD TO NET ZERO

A net-zero transition refers to the process of reducing GHG (greenhouse gas) emissions to a level where any remaining emissions are offset by removing an equivalent amount of carbon from the atmosphere, resulting in a net-zero balance. This means that the amount of GHG emissions produced by human activities is equal to the amount that is removed from the atmosphere through natural or artificial means, such as reforestation or carbon capture technology.

The net-zero transition is a crucial component of global efforts to mitigate climate change and limit its impact on the planet. It requires significant changes in the way we produce and consume energy, transport goods, and people, and manage natural resources. This transition involves transitioning away from fossil fuels to renewable energy sources, improving energy efficiency, and implementing circular economy models that reduce waste and resource consumption.

To achieve a net-zero transition, governments, businesses, and individuals need to collaborate and work toward a common goal. This involves setting targets, developing strategies, and implementing policies and measures that support the transition to a net-zero economy. This includes investing in research and development of new technologies, creating incentives for low-carbon investments, and promoting sustainable lifestyles and consumption patterns.

Overall, a net-zero transition is a necessary step toward a more sustainable future, and it requires significant effort and commitment from all sectors of society (Maynard & Abdulla, 2023). As we have mentioned, a very relevant difference between net zero and low carbon is the level of ambition. Net zero is a more ambitious goal than low carbon because it requires not only reducing emissions but also removing any remaining emissions from the atmosphere. Achieving net zero is a crucial step in mitigating climate change and limiting its impact on the planet.

OTHER FORMS OF INNOVATION

Venture philanthropy (Frumkin, 2004) takes the best practices from venture capital and philanthropy in order to approach more risky endeavors. Venture philanthropy can also be called venture investments or venture capital. As venture capital, this application takes a risky investment and makes a numbers game to try to potentialize the potential of success for a single project to finance the risk of a number of unsuccessful tries.

Venture capital is another area where SF can have an interesting scope of potential. Early-stage companies with a very high return and impact potential can be ideal for it. Venture capital is trendy because of its promise. A typical example can be an entrepreneur with a great idea that goes to a financial institution and pitches an idea. They get some money, let's say US$1,000,000, to keep it around, or even more depending on what the potential investors find in that particular pitch. If things go well, investors will get more than that million back in return. The company that is behind that pitched idea with great potential can prove its worth and return much more than that as soon as it hits the market. But on the downside, there is always the possibility that something goes wrong, and even good ideas can underperform in a bad market or under bad implementation.

Statistically, some companies will do great and outperform, and some will never make it. That, in the end, is a numbers game, and as soon as you have enough companies in the pool, and some sort of sensibility of choosing the right companies, you can expect an overall positive result. Meaning that those companies that do well pay for the risk of the other companies in your portfolio that did not perform. That, of course, relies on the fact that those companies that perform do extremely well, but if we think about those companies called "unicorns," we would get the idea. Unicorns are startup companies that reach a value of over a billion dollars. We use such a metaphorical term because of how uncommon, even impossible, successfully finding one would be.

I am sure you have several companies in mind for this category at this point. But we should keep in mind that for every unicorn, there are thousands of unsuccessful companies that did not make it and will never make it. And that is why venture capital is regarded as risky. But remember, in Finance, we do not really avoid risk; we deal with it. In the case of venture capital, we find the right price for it; after all, it is a numbers game. We can also incorporate impact in the metrics. We can also find interesting ways to implement the best practices of venture capital. A lot of different environmental and social impact activities can be included there. This is venture philanthropy, but it also goes by other names. It also can be called philanthrocapitalism, effective altruism, etc. Some other examples of innovation in SF can be found in Figure 13.5.

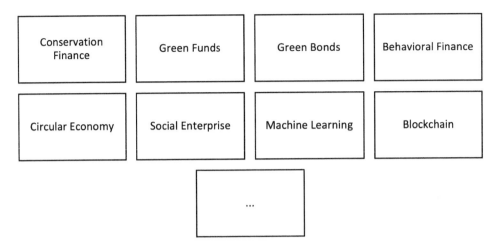

FIGURE 13.5 Some more examples of potential innovation in SF.

EVOLUTION OF GENERATIVE AI AND OTHER TECHNOLOGY

Why don't we check what happens when we ask ChatGPT[8] to describe its own advantages toward SF? Perhaps we can come up with a text like the one included here.

As an A.I. language model, ChatGPT can help promote sustainable finance in several ways:

1 *Educating people: ChatGPT can provide accurate and up-to-date information about sustainable finance, its importance, and its benefits. This can help raise awareness and understanding of sustainable finance among the general public.*
2 *Offering guidance: ChatGPT can provide guidance and advice on sustainable finance strategies and investments, based on the user's preferences and risk tolerance. This can help individuals make informed decisions about their investments and support the transition to a low-carbon economy.*
3 *Providing analysis: ChatGPT can analyze financial data and provide insights on the sustainability performance of companies and industries. This can help investors and other stakeholders make informed decisions about their investments and encourage companies to improve their sustainability practices.*
4 *Supporting research: ChatGPT can assist researchers in identifying trends, patterns, and opportunities in sustainable finance. This can contribute to the development of new sustainable finance solutions and strategies.*
5 *Facilitating communication: ChatGPT can facilitate communication between stakeholders in sustainable finance, such as investors, companies, policymakers, and NGOs. This can help promote collaboration and collective action towards a sustainable future.*

Overall, ChatGPT can play an essential role in promoting sustainable finance by providing accurate information, offering guidance, providing analysis, supporting research, and facilitating communication between stakeholders.

ChatGPT Monday, March 6, 2023, 13:08 CET (OpenAI, 2022)

Or what if we ask it to create a similar text with an ironic tone? And we get this:

> *Ah, sustainable finance. The practice of investing in companies that prioritize environmental, social, and governance issues. It's like the latest fad diet, everyone's doing it and it's supposed to make you feel better about yourself, but does it really?*
>
> *Let's face it, investing is all about making money. And sustainable finance is no different. It's just a fancy way of saying "let's invest in companies that are less likely to get sued for environmental disasters and human rights violations."*
>
> *Sure, it's great to invest in companies that are committed to reducing their carbon footprint and treating their employees fairly, but let's not pretend that this is some kind of selfless act. We're doing it because it makes us feel good and it's good for our bottom line.*
>
> *And don't even get me started on green bonds. You know, those bonds that are supposed to fund environmentally friendly projects like wind farms and solar power plants. Sounds great, right? Except that there is no real way to verify if the money is actually going toward these projects. So, basically, we're just trusting these companies to do the right thing. Because corporations are known for their honesty and integrity, right?*
>
> *But hey, at least we're doing something, right? It's better than not doing anything at all. It's like saying, "I recycle, therefore, I'm saving the planet." Sure, it's a small step, but it's better than nothing. And that's what sustainable finance is all about, taking small steps towards a more sustainable future. It's not going to solve all of our problems, but it's a start.*
>
> *And who knows, maybe one day we'll look back and laugh at how naive we were to think that investing in companies that care about the planet was some kind of revolutionary idea. But for now, let's pat ourselves on the back for doing our part to save the world, one investment at a time.*
>
> ChatGPT Wednesday, March 8, 2023, 11:23 CET (OpenAI, 2022)

Or perhaps ask it to write some highlights on SF, i.e. including emojis, and the alternatives could go on. I suggest you give it a try; it is really fun. But the potential benefits that it can bring, and the disruption that it may bring to the financial and other industries, are expected to be massive.

IN A NUTSHELL

Innovation is essential in SF because it can help address the challenges that arise from the transition to a more sustainable global economy. SF aims to encourage investments that generate long-term value by promoting ESG factors. Innovation is crucial to achieving this goal because it can enable financial institutions and companies to develop new products, services, and business models that incorporate ESG considerations. For example, innovation can help financial institutions create more accurate ESG risk assessments, which can inform investment decisions and improve portfolio management. It can also enable the development of new financial instruments, such as green bonds, which can help channel capital toward sustainable projects.

Innovation is also essential for companies seeking to transition to more sustainable practices. By developing new technologies and business models, companies can reduce their environmental impact, improve social outcomes, and enhance their governance practices. This, in turn, can help them attract sustainable investment and improve their long-term financial performance. One of the biggest challenges ahead is uncertainty. In this world that we are living in today, we understand that there is a lot of change, but we really have no precedent for understanding where it will go.

DISCUSSION QUESTIONS

1 What is the concept of the evolution of sustainable finance, and how is it described by different authors?
2 What is the importance of stakeholder integration and value creation in sustainable finance? How can value creation for all stakeholders be achieved in sustainable finance?
3 What is the positive outcome of the COVID-19 pandemic according to the text?
4 What is "Jevon's paradox," and how does it relate to sustainability?
5 What is fintech, and why is it an exciting evolution in the financial industry?
6 What ethical and humanitarian issues should be considered in the implementation of Fintech solutions?
7 What are some examples of fintech implementations that promote social inclusion?
8 What is the "lightbulb paradox"? How does the "lightbulb paradox" relate to the concept of sustainable finance?
9 What is a net-zero transition and why is it important?
10 What is venture philanthropy, and how does it relate to sustainable finance?

NOTES

1 For further reference, please see https://www.un.org/millenniumgoals/
2 For further reference, please see https://sdgs.un.org/
3 For further information, see https://www.dw.com/en/germany-introduces-9-ticket-to-offset-the-impact-of-the-ukraine-war/a-61788020
4 For further information, see https://www.theatlantic.com/business/archive/2012/02/a-short-history-of-american-money-from-fur-to-fiat/252620/
5 M-PESA is a mobile payments and money transfer. Launched by the conglomerates Vodafone and Safaricom in 2007. For further information, please see https://www.vodafone.com/about-vodafone/what-we-do/consumer-products-and-services/m-pesa
6 For further information, please see https://www.youtube.com/watch?v=i0dBWaen3aQ
7 For further information, please see https://www.theeastafrican.co.ke/tea/business/safaricom-m-pesa-crosses-30-million-active-users-in-kenya-3743258#:~:text=The%20telco's%20chief%20executive%20Peter,2020%20to%20more%20than%20387%2C000·
8 ChatGPT is an AI chatbot from the company OpenAI and based on "Generative Pre-trained Transformer" technology for large language models. For further reference see https://chat.openai.com

WORKS CITED

Allcott, H., & Taubinsky, D. (2013). The lightbulb paradox: Evidence from two randomized experiments. *Working Paper 19713*. National Bureau of Economic Research.

Busch, T., Bruce-Clark, P., Derwall, J., Eccles, R., Hebb, T., Hoepner, A., … Weber, O. (2021). Impact investments: A call for (re) orientation. *SN Business & Economics, 1*, 33.

Edmans, A. (2021). *Grow the pie.* Cambridge University Press.

Edmans, A., Fang, V. W., & Huang, A. H. (2022). The long-term consequences of short-term incentives. *Journal of Accounting Research, 60*(3), 1007–1046.

Frumkin, P. (2004). Inside venture philanthropy. In *Search of the nonprofit sector. Society, 40(4)*, 7.

Gikunda, R. M., Abura, G. O., & Njeru, S. G. (2014). Socio-economic effects of Mpesa adoption on the livelihoods of people in Bureti Sub County, Kenya. *International Journal of Academic Research in Business and Social Sciences, 4*(12), 348.

Iqbal, S., Bilal, A. R., Nurunnabi, M., Iqbal, W., Alfakhri, Y., & Iqbal, N. (2021). It is time to control the worst: Testing COVID-19 outbreak, energy consumption and CO_2 emission. *Environmental Science and Pollution Research, 28*, 19008–19020.

Leong, K., & Sung, A. (2018). FinTech (Financial Technology): What is it and how to use technologies to create business value in fintech way? *International Journal of Innovation, Management and Technology, 9*(2), 74–78.

Maynard, I., & Abdulla, A. (2023). Assessing benefits and costs of expanded green hydrogen production to facilitate fossil fuel exit in a net-zero transition. *Renewable Energy Focus, 44*, 85–97.

Naveed, K., Watanabe, C., & Neittaanmäki, P. (2017). Co-evolution between streaming and live music leads a way to the sustainable growth of music industry – Lessons from the US experiences. *Technology in Society, 50*, 1–19.

OpenAI. (2022, March). *ChatGPT.* Retrieved from https://chat.openai.com/chat

Sachs, J. D. (2012). From millennium development goals to sustainable development goals. *The Lancelet, 379*(9832), 2206–2211.

Schoenmaker, D. (2018). A framework for sustainable finance. *SSRN Electronic Journal.* doi:10.2139/ssrn.3125351

World Economic Forum. (n.d.). *Top 10 risks global risks report 2023.* Retrieved from https://www3.weforum.org/docs/WEF_Global_Risks_Report_2023.pdf

A brief introduction to time value of money[1]

WHAT IS TIME VALUE OF MONEY?

Time value of money (TVM) is a financial concept that states that money received or paid over time has different values. According to TVM, the value of money changes due to various factors, i.e., inflation, opportunity cost, and the potential for investment returns. The TVM concept is based on the idea that money available today is worth more than the same amount of money in the future because it can be invested or used to earn returns, i.e., if you receive US$100 today, you can invest it and earn interest or returns over time, making it worth more than US$100 in the future. Similarly, if you have to pay US$100 in the future, consider the interest or returns you could have earned if you had that money today.

TVM is critical in understanding how money changes in value over time and how it can be invested or used to earn returns. TVM can be applied in various financial calculations, i.e., calculating loan payments and determining the appropriate discount rate for a project or investment. It is an essential concept in Finance because it helps individuals and organizations make informed financial decisions.

WHY IS TVM SO COMMONLY USED IN FINANCE?

The popularity of TVM is due to several reasons. First, the concept of TVM is intuitive and straightforward. Second, TVM can be applied to various financial transactions, such as investments, loans, and mortgages, making it a versatile tool for financial analysis. Third, the TVM concept provides a precise approach that accurately calculates future cash flows, present values, and interest rates. Fourth, TVM is helpful for financial planning and budgeting, as it helps individuals and organizations to forecast future cash flows and plan accordingly.

WHAT ARE THE ESSENTIAL ELEMENTS OF TVM?

There are four essential elements of TVM (Table AA.1):

TABLE AA.1 Elements of TVM

Element	Usual Abbreviation	Definition	Formula
Present value	PV	PV is the current value of money that will be received or paid in the future. PV is calculated by discounting future cash flows at a given interest rate to adjust for TVM.	$PV = FV/(1 + r)$
Future value	FV	FV is the value of an amount of money at a specified time in the future, given a specific interest rate. FV is calculated by compounding the present value at a given interest rate over a specified period.	$FV = PV/(1 + r)^n$
Time	n	The time element in TVM represents the period over which the money is invested or borrowed. TVM recognizes that the longer the time period, the more significant the impact of compounding or discounting on the value of money.	–
Interest or discount rate	r	TVM also involves the interest rate or the discount rate. The interest rate represents the cost of money or the opportunity cost of investing money in a particular project or investment. The discount rate discounts future cash flows to their present value.	–

INTEREST RATE

An interest rate is the amount charged or paid for using money over a specific period, expressed as a percentage of the amount borrowed or invested. In other words, it is the cost of borrowing or the return on investment. There are two types of interest rates: nominal interest rates and real interest rates. On the one hand, nominal interest rates are the rates that are quoted by banks and financial institutions and do not account for inflation. On the other hand, real interest rates adjust for inflation and provide a more accurate measure of the cost of borrowing or the return on investment. Interest rates can vary depending on a variety of factors.

Interest rates play a crucial role in the economy and affect various financial transactions, such as loans, mortgages, and investments. For borrowers, higher interest rates can increase the cost of borrowing, making it more challenging to repay the loan. For investors, higher interest rates can provide a higher return on investment and increase the risk of losses. Understanding interest rates is essential for individuals and organizations to make informed financial decisions.

WHY IS IT CHALLENGING TO INCORPORATE INTEREST RATES INTO SUSTAINABLE FINANCE?

Incorporating interest rates into sustainable finance (SF) can be challenging because sustainability considerations can affect the traditional economic assumptions that underlie interest rate calculations, i.e., long-term thinking, externalities, uncertainty, and intangible value, among others. These elements have been described in different chapters of this book.

OTHER VALUATION METHODS

Although TVM might be one of the most popular valuation methodologies, it is not the only valuation method in Finance. Several other valuation methods are commonly used in Finance, depending on the specific context and type of financial asset being valued. For further reference, see Chapter 2.

THE USE OF TVM IN SF

While the concept of TVM is widely used in financial decision-making, it can be challenging to use it in SF. Here are some reasons:

ESG (environmental, social, and governance) factors: TVM calculations typically rely on financial data solely, such as interest rates and cash flows, but SF requires the consideration of ESG factors that affect the financial performance of investments. These factors may not be easily quantifiable in a way that can be included in TVM calculations.

Long-term perspective: SF often takes a long-term perspective. TVM calculations are usually based on shorter time horizons.

Uncertainty: SF involves dealing with uncertainty, such as the impact of climate change on investments. TVM calculations assume predictability and linearity.

Complex systems: SF often involves complex systems, i.e., ecosystems. TVM is not the best fit to model complexity.

CONCLUSIONS

TVM is commonly used in Finance due to its simplicity, versatility, accuracy, and usefulness in financial planning and analysis. It is a fundamental principle in Finance widely used in various financial applications, making it an essential tool for financial decision-making. The use of TVM in SF, however, can be complex, provided the above-mentioned reasons, and more research is still needed to improve the implementation of TVM in SF. While TVM is a useful financial concept, its limitations make it challenging to use in SF.

NOTE

1 Regarding concepts introduced in this chapter, the author's explanation is designed to be sufficient to provide a clear and concise yet general and summarized understanding of TVM and its importance in Finance. This is not meant to be an exhaustive description, and further information can be found in other sources listed in this section or available in other sources.

DISCUSSION QUESTIONS

1 What is time value of money?
2 How does time value of money impact financial transactions?
3 What are the essential elements of time value of money, and how are they calculated?
4 What is the role of interest rates in financial transactions?
5 Why is incorporating TVM into SF challenging? What needs to be considered?

A brief introduction to financial statements[1]

WHAT IS A FINANCIAL STATEMENT?

A financial statement is a document that summarizes the financial activities of a company or an individual. Financial statements provide an overview of the financial performance and position of a company or an individual. They are used to make financial decisions and evaluate the financial health of an organization.

WHAT ARE THE PRIMARY FINANCIAL STATEMENTS?[2]

Financial statements typically include the balance sheet, income statement, and cash flow statement, (Table AB.1) providing a comprehensive view of a company's financial health.

CONCLUSIONS

The main financial statements comprehensively view a company's financial performance, position, and cash flows. They are used by investors, analysts, and other stakeholders to evaluate a company's financial health, profitability, and growth prospects.

By analyzing financial statements, investors and analysts can make informed decisions about investing in a company. For example, they may look at a company's profitability, liquidity, and solvency ratios to assess its financial health and determine whether it is a good investment. Additionally, financial statements are essential for companies, as they can use the information to identify areas for improvement and make strategic decisions about their operations and finances.

DISCUSSION QUESTIONS

1   What is the purpose of financial statements?
2   What are the primary financial statements?
3   How does an income statement differ from a balance sheet?

TABLE AB.1 Main financial statements

Financial Statements	Description
Income statement	An income statement, also known as a profit and loss statement, summarizes a company's revenues, expenses, and profits or losses over a specific period, typically a month, a quarter, or a year.
Balance sheet	A balance sheet provides a snapshot of a company's financial position at a specific time. It lists the company's assets, liabilities, and equity and shows how the company's assets are financed.
Cash flow statement	A cash flow statement provides information about a company's inflows and outflows of cash over a specific period. It shows how much cash a company generates from its operations, how much it invests in assets, and how much it raises or repays in debt and equity.
Statement of changes in equity	This statement shows how a company's equity has changed over a specific period. It includes information on share capital, retained earnings, and other equity-related transactions.

4 Why are financial statements important for investors and analysts?
5 How can companies use financial statements to make strategic decisions about their operations and finances?

NOTES

1 Regarding concepts introduced in this chapter, the author's explanation is designed to be sufficient to provide a clear and concise yet general and summarized understanding of financial statements. This is not meant to be an exhaustive description, and further information can be found in other sources listed in this section or available in other sources.
2 For further information, go to Investopedia (2022).

Index